"Bravo, Amerikanski!"

and Other Stories

from World War II

"Bravo, Amerikanski!"

and Other Stories

from World War II

by

Ann Stringer

As Told to Mark Scott

With an Introduction by
Walter Cronkite

1st Books Rev. 6/26/00

About the book

Ann Stringer was the most glamorous woman correspondent of World War II. The ravishingly beautiful Texan accompanied US troops on their drive into Nazi Germany, was the first reporter to enter the liberated Nordhausen concentration camp, and got the scoop on the biggest story of the war--the linkup of US and Soviet armies at the Elbe River. United Press considered Ann Stringer its star reporter.

"She was tough. She knew what she wanted, and she knew how to get it. And she was one of the best reporters I have ever known. And, yes, she was beautiful."

--Walter Cronkite

"Bill Stringer, killed in Normandy, was replaced on the job by his wife, Ann. The rest of us in the First Army press camp didn't know how to act toward her. Ann made it easy. She just picked up and did Bill's job, often with tears in her eyes."

--Andy Rooney

"What I can tell you about her is that she was simply superb, the best *man* (I'll say that even if it sounds chauvinistic) on the staff. Annie illuminated every one of her assignments. She was all reporter--not "girl reporter"-- straight reporter. She was a two-fisted competitor."

--Harrison Salisbury

"When the next century closes out, I wouldn't bet that someone won't be writing about her then as I have now."

--Col. Barney Oldfield

"When is Ann Stringer of the United Press coming back? She had the most beautiful legs in Romania."

--Petru Groza
Prime Minister of Romania

"Aside from the horrors of war, it was an exciting time. We were living to the hilt--of our capabilities, of our senses, and of our energy."

--Ann Stringer

Dedicated to the Memory of

William John Stringer, Jr.

PERMISSIONS

Walter Cronkite introduction copyright © 1999 by Walter Cronkite.

Photographs "United Press war correspondent Ann Stringer, 1945" and "Reuters war correspondent William Jr. Stringer, Jr." courtesy Burlington-Rock Island Railroad Museum, Teague. Texas.

Ann Stringer's account of her meeting with Soviet troops at Torgau, Germany, from Mark Scott and Semyon Krasilshchik, eds., *Yanks Meet Reds: Recollections of US and Soviet Vets from the Linkup in World War II.* Santa Barbara: Capra Press, 1988. Copyright © 1988 by Mark Scott.

SPECIAL THANKS TO:

Peter Branton, National Timberwolf Association, Wichita, Kansas.

Walter Cronkite, New York, New York.

Bernard Edinger, Reuters France, Paris, France.

John Entwisle, The Reuters Archive, London, United Kingdom.

Ginny Folsom, Burlington-Rock Island Railroad Museum, Teague, Texas.

Allan Jackson, Pensacola, Florida.

W. H. McSpadden, Burlington-Rock Island Railroad Museum, Teague, Texas.

National Archives, Washington, D. C.

Col. Barney Oldfield, The Col. Barney Oldfield Organization, Inc., Beverly Hills, California.

Gordon Riess, Intercontinental Enterprises Limited, Beverly Hills, California.

MCS

CONTENTS

Introduction

I never had the honor, pleasure or, perhaps, discomfort of meeting Ann Stringer during the fighting. We were with different units at different times.

But I heard a lot about her. Her fame--as a beauty, a personality and a ruthlessly competitive correspondent--had spread from press camp to press camp along the entire Western front. Her determination to be first with the big story not infrequently brought her into conflict with her own colleagues in the United Press and created thorny jurisdictional problems for her immediate bosses.

When I took over as UP's chief correspondent at the Nuernberg trials of Goering, Hess, Ribbentrop *et al*[1], I found Annie as one of my reportorial corps. I girded for trouble.

The story there was, of course, the daily trial, but the most sensational material was that still locked in the files of the Third Reich, the *Wehrmacht*[2], the *Luftwaffe*[3] and the Navy. The Allies had seized them all and most of them were under heavy guard right there in the courthouse.

Those files held the stories, never before told, of the genesis of the pogroms against the Jews, of the founding of the concentration camps and the gas chambers, of Hitler's decision to call off the *Luftwaffe's* offensive against Britain on the eve of possible victory, of the Navy's U-boat campaign in the North Atlantic and machine-gunning of lifeboats crowded with civilians.

The biggest stories were in those files, but neither the defendants' lawyers nor correspondents were privileged to rifle through them. We had to ask specifically for a single document, and the Allied powers vetted our requests.

Finding out what documents to ask for was the key to the reportorial game. This required a lot of contacts, both with the Allied prosecution and the German defense, and then hours of discreet, diplomatic, clever probing--in the halls of the courthouse, at cocktails or dinner.

Annie was an absolute whiz at it. Day after day she came up with a new document recounting the behind the scenes workings of the Nazi state and the horrors it perpetrated. Day after day we had clear scoops and, happily, the opposition was confounded. It was a bureau manager's delight.

And Annie was so far ahead of the rest of us at this game, that within UP there was never any cause for jealousy or the wars over turf that can plague a manager's life.

The only problem I had with her was when the stories of the full horror of Nazism, their shock value expended, began to move from the front page to the back of the papers. With that Ann got nervous and began demanding to move on to a more active scene, even while she still was producing great and exclusive material. That was a fight I was bound to lose, and I could have saved both of us a lot of grief if I had been sensible enough to realize that a lot earlier.

She was tough. She knew what she wanted, and she knew how to get it. And she was one of the best reporters I have ever known. And, yes, she was beautiful.

Walter Cronkite

CHAPTER ONE

Eastland, Airplanes, and Bill

It wasn't so long ago, was it?[4] Bill's sudden death on that deserted country road in France. That day I walked alone under enemy shellfire across the Remagen Bridge so I could get the story on the other side. The rotting human flesh of Nordhausen, the "Bitch of Buchenwald," and that young Russian soldier in Torgau--wearing nothing but a cap and pair of undershorts--spotting Allan Jackson and me and yelling, *"Bravo, Amerikanski! Bravo,* Comrades!" Interviews with Mussolini's widow and the Pope. A defiant Rudolf Hess in the dock at Nuremberg arrogantly shouting *"Nein!"* and Nijinsky in Vienna eating the peanut butter I'd gotten him from the American mess. Hundreds of starving Berliners scouring the streets in search of their only meal--acorns. Helga Soest in the trunk of my Buick as we drove past Russian guards to Tempelhof. In Istanbul, playing jokes on the Turkish secret police. No, it wasn't so very long ago. It always seems like only yesterday.

I'd always wanted to be a writer. I guess I had always had that interest, even when I was a child. But it was Mother who pushed me into getting started. That was in Texas, where I grew up, went to college, and married Bill.

I was born Elizabeth Ann Harrell in Eastland, Texas, on December 9, 1918. Eastland is a small town located between Abilene and Fort Worth, near Ranger. It is the county seat, and was the center of the Texas oil boom. My father, Thomas Coleman Harrell, was in the oil business, although he had grown up on a farm in west Texas, been a schoolteacher for a short time, and then served as county tax collector. The year before I was born, Daddy had started buying up farm land around Eastland. It just so happened that the land he owned was sitting on oil. People would come to him asking permission to drill for oil on his property. And so he soon started drilling oil for himself, and was very successful at it.

When oil was just discovered, Daddy was not earning a great deal of money. By the early twenties, the value of his property was appraised at about seven million dollars, which was a great deal of money then--it still is. Daddy was an entrepreneur, open to all kinds of things. He owned the Tom Harrell Lumber Company, which had seven yards, and was president of five banks. And he gave a lot of money away, to churches and schools.

When I was young--in my early teens--Daddy and I didn't go for any strolls in the woods, anything like that, because there were places he had to be. The two of us would go driving in his car to the oil fields. He'd be checking on a well being drilled. When I visited the oil fields with him, all the men there treated me well, although they were always pretty busy. I suppose that even as a girl I became accustomed to being around men at work.

I remember that whenever Daddy went out to see a well come in, he would wear a new suit. And if the well was a gusher, the suit would always be ruined. But, of course, the oil more than paid for a new one. It did so until 1929, when Daddy lost everything in the Depression, everything but what he had given away. He later said, "If I hadn't given that money away, it too would have gone down the hole. Those contributions were the only thing I saved."

Daddy remained in the oil business, servicing oil field equipment. By the time of his death, he had repaid all the debts left over from the days when business had not been good.

My mother, Bernie Harrell, was originally from Lipan, Texas. She too came from a farm family and, like Daddy, had also taught elementary school. After they were married, she gave up teaching, became a housewife, and reared a family. Besides myself, there was my sister, Mary Jane, three years younger than I. Then there was Thomas-- Thomas Coleman, Jr.--and my little brother, Robert Bruce Harrell--Bobby. But mother wasn't just a humdrum housewife. She was active in the church, the Church of Christ. That took up much of her time, along with running the home. She enjoyed reading, and when she thought I wanted to write, encouraged me to do so.

It was mother who taught me to cook. I was always considered a good cook. This knowledge came in very handy after the war when I was a photographic assistant. As a girl, I was in the Campfire Girls, things like that. Played the piano. Went to dances and football games. I dated many boys when I was in high school, but not several at one time. I read a lot--Ernest Hemingway, Sherwood Anderson, Willa Cather, James Joyce, William Faulkner, John Dos Passos, Gertrude Stein, Eugene O'Neill. My favorite motion picture actor was Clark Gable. I also liked Vivien Leigh and Katherine Hepburn.

I wasn't as religious as Mother, and became even less so after I left home. I was never attracted to the mysticism

5

of religion, never thought I had a guardian angel. And the Church of Christ was so narrow-minded. I didn't turn my back on religion, but thought that a narrow religion could cause a lot of hurt. If other people believe in something that doesn't cause harm to others, why be against it?

After Daddy struck oil--when I was sixteen--the family moved from Eastland to Tyler, and later to Kilgore. After graduating from Tyler High School in 1936, I attended a business school and enrolled at Tyler Junior College. I received a degree in shorthand from the business school the following year. This skill later came in handy, because when I was a reporter, I always took notes in shorthand. I went to Tyler Junior College for a year. Able to type and take shorthand, I then decided to move to Dallas, where I got a job through a friend with the Dies Committee.

Working with the Dies Committee was interesting, although I was only a secretary. As you may recall, the Dies Committee was looking for Communists and that sort of thing. It was very reactionary. We were examining many bigshots. I have no particular memory of Congressman Martin Dies himself. He was always so tied up in what he was doing. But many of the people I worked with on the Committee were rednecks and fanatics of various sorts. That came partly from their religious fundamentalism, partly from their small-town, provincial outlook. Despite that, my work with the Committee was interesting because it was a different kind of life. It sparked my interest in political subjects, it surely did. It pushed me toward journalism. And so after working with the Dies Committee for a couple of months, I decided to go back to school, this time to Southern Methodist University right there in Dallas.

At SMU, I studied journalism. This in itself wasn't all that unusual, since many women were studying journalism along with me. I think that because Texas was a western state rather than a southern state, it may have been more socially acceptable for me as a woman to be studying journalism than if I had been going to college in the Deep South. I don't recall that my male professors encouraged me in any particular way, that they treated me any differently than the male students. They certainly didn't tell me that journalism wasn't a profession for women. Remember, everything was risky for a woman to go into then except the home and kitchen. I wasn't told I wouldn't have a great future in journalism. I wasn't promised any great future, but I had decided I was going into it--period. I had come to love journalism. It allowed a person to be independent, creative, and persistent, all of which made it especially attractive to me.

I stayed at SMU only a short time, having decided to continue my journalism studies at the University of Texas in Austin. It was a larger school and there were many more opportunities there. I don't remember many women from small towns attending the University of Texas at the time. I guess we were a little bit special because we were from small towns and were female.

By that time, Daddy's business had fallen on hard times. So I got a job in the university library to pay my keep and tuition. Mother and Daddy didn't force it upon me, but I knew that times were bad, that there were other children in the family, and felt I should pull my own weight. I felt that money or no money, I should be independent. My library job paid 35¢ an hour, but I could work as many hours as I wanted, with duties that included checking books in and out and putting them back on the shelves. And I had ways of cutting corners, saving money while working at the library. Rather than buying food, I'd often try to "fool" my digestive tract by drinking water and chewing rubber bands. I could chew the rubber bands as much as I wanted while thinking I was really eating. This was a meal I could afford--I could chew the same rubber bands for the next "meal." Thirty-five cents didn't go far then, even if you worked many hours. But my interest in working at the library was more than money. I was surrounded by so many interesting ideas. Very likely, I could have earned more as a waitress. And then eating has never been that important to me. I was always being nagged to eat more. I was always known for drinking Cokes for breakfast.

As a student at the University of Texas, I devoted most of my time to my schoolwork, with not a great deal of social life. I took as many courses as were permitted-- twenty-one hours a semester--and had to get special permission from my adviser to do that. Students generally took an eighteen-hour course load. My favorite courses were in journalism, English, and history. The foreign language I studied was Latin, which was surprisingly useful when I went to Romania just after the war. Studying these subjects opened my eyes to the fact that almost anything is a story if handled correctly--personalities, events. It may have been my professors in the classroom who helped open my eyes to it.

But still, I didn't spend all my time in the classroom. Most of the people I ran around with were journalists of a sort. For about a year, I took flying lessons. They might have saved me one time in Romania when we ran out of gas while flying over Transylvania. Well, I was the only woman in my particular group. I learned to fly because it was just something I wanted to do. It was expensive, but fun and interesting. I was flying a small plane. I don't remember what kind. It seems we used the municipal airport there in Austin. I usually flew with one of the men, but there were times when I soloed. All of us used to walk around campus in flying formation--with our arms out-- pretending to be planes.

The men didn't discourage me from taking flying lessons. There was no barrier I can recall. There was just the feeling that everyone was entitled to do what he or she wanted to do. My male instructors didn't think that my taking lessons was all that unusual. From an early age, my working relationship with men had been this way--positive and supportive. I didn't feel as if I were constantly fighting them. There was almost a camaraderie. I didn't ask men for special favors, or loopholes, or anything. I think that made it easier for them to accept me.

Then I met Bill. I don't remember exactly when it was. It may have been in the classroom or at some extracurricular event. Bill Stringer was a journalism student. He was from Teague, Texas. His father, William J. Stringer, Sr., was editor of the *Teague Chronicle*. Mr. Stringer's assistant was Bill's mother.

Bill and I had similar backgrounds and similar goals, although we may not have known it when we first met. He was good looking, bright, delightful, fun to be around, had a wonderful sense of humor, and was wide open as far as his interests--and mine--were concerned. He tended to be more critical of people, whereas I was inclined to overlook their faults. He wanted me to be all that I could be, always encouraging me to be independent.

We understood each other. I guess you'd say that both of us were workaholics. But the wonderful thing about our work was that it was all play.

We were married during our senior year at college. We knew we were going to get married not long after we met. I don't recall any formal proposal. There was no engagement. It was just sort of understood, something in the works--on both sides. We just recognized that it was inevitable. We shared many things, so many things. Everything, in fact.

We were married at my parents' home in Kilgore on March 2, 1940. It was private--just family. His parents came over from Teague. A more formal wedding would have been just for show, and neither of us wanted that. It wasn't a church wedding because we wanted something that would be the easiest, simplest, quickest. We didn't need any big celebration, because we had each other. That was all we really needed. There was no honeymoon. We just went back to school.

We graduated in June of 1940. I received two bachelor degrees, one in Journalism and the other in English. And then we moved to Dallas, where he joined up with United Press and I got a job writing copy for an ad agency until I could get something with a newspaper. Shortly after that, UP transferred him to Columbus, Ohio, where he was made Bureau Manager. So that's how I left Texas. Going to Columbus was the first time in my life I'd been out of Texas. It meant seeing how other parts of the world lived. Columbus was the state capital, and was certainly larger than Eastland, Kilgore, or Teague.

In Columbus, UP also offered me a job. I joined with some hesitation, because I was afraid that my working for UP might hold Bill back, hurt his career. But he insisted, saying that since they offered me the job I should take it. As Unipressers, Bill and I tried to separate our marriage relationship from the office. But whenever he would walk past me in the office, he'd give me a little thump, and I'd know it was he, and didn't even have to look around. I miss that yet today.

Bill thought that my working for UP was something else we could do together. That's the way our marriage was. Not competitive. There wasn't any jealousy. We were a team, but didn't work as a team.

CHAPTER TWO

Inside the Juelich Citadel

In 1943, UP gave Bill and me a new assignment--
South America. And so we left Columbus for Argentina--
Buenos Aires. For about a year, we covered life in the
Argentine capital. It was a large, international city, much
larger than any city I had ever known, filled with many
interesting people.

Well, neither of us liked it. In fact, the dislike Bill and I
developed for the Argentine people, not just the leaders,
was mutual and increasing. Argentina was a rich country,
and the other South American countries were relatively
poor. The Argentines didn't speak the same language of
the other Spanish-speaking countries on the continent, but
spoke *castillano*--Castilian. I thought then that wealth and
tradition was the main reason for the Argentine conceit. It
wasn't a political thing. It wasn't Italian fascism, which
was so popular there. I didn't feel the same way about the
Italians when I later lived in Rome. I didn't feel the same
way about other South Americans. When Bill and I visited
Chile, Brazil, Peru, it was a wonderful breath of fresh air.
The people were so open, so different from the Argentines.

But the Argentines were very arrogant, very superior to anyone, anywhere. In fact, they were the most arrogant people I've ever met, more arrogant than the Germans. The Argentines may have been this way even more so with Americans because they could have felt that Americans--many of whom were also rich and powerful--posed more of a threat to them, and for this reason had to be particularly snubbed. Because of this unbelievable arrogance, I thought at the time that Argentina was especially suited to fascism of some sort.

The military takeover of the country in June 1943 wasn't really a big surprise to either Bill or me. There had been a feeling of unrest for some time in Buenos Aires. On June 4, army officers led by Minister of War Gen. Pedro Ramirez and Gen. Antonio Rawson quickly ousted President Ramon Castillo in an almost bloodless coup. Within a short time, Rawson issued a decree proclaiming martial law for all of Argentina.

In Buenos Aires itself, intense gunfire broke out for a time in the Plaza de Mayo when milling crowds staged a demonstration in front of Government House, where Ramirez and Rawson were staying. The police only had to fire about fifteen shots in the air to break up a crowd of five hundred demonstrators. Protesters also stormed the offices of the pro-Axis[5] newspaper *Cabildo*, which was at the edge of the Plaza de Mayo. Other demonstrators threw rocks at the pro-fascist newspaper *Momento Argentina*. Many German businesses were stoned. There was a lot of shouting, marching in the streets, crowds with anti-Axis sentiments overturning cars and setting them on fire while shouting in Castilian, "How beautiful the burning cars!"

While all of this was going on, Castillo had fled with his cabinet to the government mine sweeper *Drummond*, anchored in the nearby Plata River. From there, he radioed the Argentine Supreme Court that he and his government were on the ship, and that they would put down the uprising. But the air force soon joined the army. And then the navy--which had at first been loyal to the President-- also joined the revolutionaries. Castillo and his Cabinet soon sailed on the *Drummond* for the safety of Uruguayan waters.

Bill and I were somewhat apprehensive after the coup, which eventually brought the government of fascist Juan Peron to power. We didn't know what measures the new leaders might take against us. They were free to do whatever they wished. But they left us alone. Gen. Rawson himself was said to have pro-Allied sentiments, particularly after the German defeats in North Africa. There were also reports that he wanted to get American lend-lease equipment.

By that time, of course, the war was the big story, bigger by far than Argentina. So Bill and I asked to return to America in the hopes of getting assigned to Europe as war correspondents. In early 1944, we arrived in New York, where we began work at the UP bureau there. Assigned to the cable desk, I was the only woman in the office. Charlie McCann, who was in charge of the cable desk, wasn't too pleased with my being there. He was famous for his profane language, and I, being a woman, cramped his style. Someone in the office told me about Charlie's attitude. And so a little later, when Charlie gave me a story to rewrite, I pretended to be having problems with my typewriter and said loud enough for him to hear, "What is it with this goddamn machine? I can't get the son-of-a-bitch-ribbon out!"

Charlie and I got along beautifully after that.

In the meantime, Bill kept trying to get sent over to Europe for the coming D-Day invasion. UP was sort of dragging its feet, so he contacted Reuters, which was looking for American correspondents to attract American readership.   In February 1944, Reuters hired him as assistant chief of its New York bureau. Within months, it sent him to Europe. The understanding was that Reuters would also send me just as soon as possible.

Having obtained his accreditation to the First Army, Bill left by plane for London in late May 1944. I remember what a lovely day it was when I saw him off at Idlewilde Airport. His was an exciting, dangerous assignment, but neither one of us thought he might actually be killed. You just don't think that way. And when he left, both of us felt I would be joining him soon. We weren't planning a long separation. When I reported to work at the cable desk on D-Day morning--June 6--I was handed a sheaf of cables. One of them was from Unipresser Jimmy McGlincy, who added at the end of his cable, "Bill sends love." So I knew he had made it safely through the D-Day landings. He had gone ashore with the first wave of the First Army on the beaches of Normandy. From there, he wanted to get to Paris.   In fact, he wanted to be the *first* Allied correspondent to re-enter Paris. He'd already been the first in Cherbourg. His stories were winning him high praise from Reuters.   "Congratulations top flight despatches getting magnificent play here and America," Reuters London News Manager Walton Cole wrote him on June 12. "Magnificent work," Cole added two weeks later. "You consistently in front."

Reuters correspondent William J. Stringer, Jr. in 1944, and
United Press correspondent Ann Stringer in 1945.
(Burlington-Rock Island Railroad Museum, Teague, Texas)

It took me some time to get my accreditation from the
Army, which wasn't very receptive to the idea of women
correspondents. And so my accreditation process took a
long time. There was a lot of red tape. They let you know
that because you were a woman you were suspect. Yes,
there was prejudice. The Army emphasized the problems
that would be created by having women serving with it, that
we would have to have special living quarters, special
latrines, etc. They made it sound very logical. I can't tell
you what they were really thinking. Nurses were needed,
but the Army didn't feel correspondents were needed,
women correspondents in particular. Fortunately, Gen.
Eisenhower was on our side, very supportive of war
correspondents--male and female. He knew we had a story
to tell, a big story, which the American people wanted to
hear. I think the Army finally realized that correspondents
could serve its purposes by reporting its victories and so

forth. All the same, it still thought that reporting was a man's job and a man's privilege. The war was a big story to be saved for the men. But I knew I could write the pants off any man. I was determined to go. And so, at last, I received my accreditation as a Reuters correspondent, and booked passage to England.

My boat was scheduled to leave New York for London on a Thursday in September 1944. Three days before my departure, I reported to work at the Reuters bureau in New York. Not long after I got there, the bureau manager called me into his office, welcomed me, and made all kinds of small talk. I was a little irritated, impatient to get to work. Then we were interrupted by a phone call for me, and so I went out to get it.

The call was from a colleague in London, Bill Higginbotham. He said, "I hope this isn't true."

"I told you all along that I was going to leave UP to work for Reuters," I replied.

"No, that's not it," he said. "Bill's been killed."

When he said that, my immediate reaction was to get over there and get there fast to be as close to Bill as possible, even though I knew he was already dead.

How had it happened? On August 17, Bill, Pvt. Lawrence Sabin (the driver), and Acme News photographer Andy Lopez were riding in a jeep, advancing on Paris with the First Army. Bill was sitting in the back seat, the rear left. I never knew why he always preferred to sit there. At the time, the three of them were way behind enemy lines searching for a command post near the front. The military police, not knowing that Germans had returned to the vicinity, told them the road was clear to the village of Dreux and farther east. Near Dreux, which is located about sixty miles west of Paris, they saw a burned-out jeep at the side of the road, and stopped to find out what was going on. "We slowed down," Andy later told me, "and there was a terrible explosion. We hadn't even heard a gun fired. I looked around and saw that Bill was hit. He never knew what had hit him."

Close by, the Germans had been using an anti-aircraft gun as an artillery piece, pointing its barrel horizontally. They had fired at the jeep, the vehicle was hit, and so was Bill. The shell didn't explode. That was the only reason the other two in the jeep weren't killed as well. The shell had hit Bill over the heart and gone right through. He was not mangled. It was over in an instant.

Andy was able to get Bill out of the jeep and onto the side of the road, where he wasn't such a target. But Andy already knew there was no hope.

Both Andy and Pvt. Sabin had been slightly wounded by shrapnel. They jumped into a ditch, then crawled on their hands and knees for a half a mile as the Germans were shelling them. They hid in the woods for thirty-six hours with nothing to eat or drink, with enemy troops moving in ever closer. Finally, they made a run back to the Allied lines. As they were feeling their way in the dark, they were stopped by the *Maquis*, the French underground. Because the *Maquis* was on our side, the two Americans were glad to see them. They clearly identified themselves as *Maquis*. Then one of the Frenchmen, for no apparent reason, shot and killed Pvt. Sabin.

Andy returned alone to the press camp and told everyone about Bill's death. Word spread to another press camp, where a doughboy woke Unipresser Johnny Mecklin and said, "You were a friend of Stringer's, weren't you? Well, he's been killed."

Johnny and Reuters correspondent John Wilhelm, whom Bill had also known, then snatched a jeep and started out immediately for Bill's press camp. There they met Andy Lopez and talked to him. Andy told them that Bill had been just outside Verneuil-sur-Avre, near a wide curve in the road at the point from which you could just see the town church spire. Johnny and Wilhelm set out.

They found three bodies in the ditch on the right hand side of the road. One was that of an American officer, the other a Frenchman. The third was covered with a blanket. Johnny said the third body was wearing paratroop boots. For this reason, they didn't think it was Bill. But on closer examination, they saw his correspondent's insignia, then found his dog tag nearby. The tag had a tiny splotch of blood on it. They knew then it was Bill, although by that time--some five days after his death--they couldn't recognize him. His cap had been placed by the Germans beside the body of the American officer. Johnny and Wilhelm took the cap and put it beside Bill.

Then the two drove on into Verneuil, just a little more than half a mile away, and drank to Bill. That was what he would have wanted them to do. And being his friends, they knew he would have wanted it. They reported the details of Bill's death to the American Army officials and personally saw to it that he was buried properly. The Army buried him with full military honors at an Army cemetery at--I was originally told--Brezolles, a village about fifteen miles west of Dreux.

Johnny told me that the place where Bill died was beautiful, peaceful countryside belying the horror and death it had witnessed only days before. The skies were clear and blue that day, the weather fine. Wide, rolling pasture lands stretched from both sides of the road. In the distance, off to one side, was a little forest beyond the fields. Along the left side of the road, on the way to Verneuil, was a row of trees. In one place, just at the curve, there was a small gap in the trees and hedgerows. Bill's body had been just opposite that gap, on the far side of the road.

My husband was only twenty-seven years old. He had died at the very peak of his career, when everything was going so well, so fast. He was within a few miles of the biggest story of his life, the liberation of Paris, the city he loved and which we had planned for so many years to visit together. He was happy. Andy said that on the morning of his death all Bill could talk about was getting to Paris ahead of everyone else, getting the story, and getting me over there. How we would have celebrated![6] Johnny took a photograph of the spot where Bill had died, and sent it to me. Later, he and Wilhelm went up the road and found the gun which had hit him. By then, it had been captured and put out of action.

Four days after Bill's death, his Reuters pal Bob Reuben composed an open letter to Bill--in memory of him. The letter read in part:

> We were reminiscing about you and your famous escapades last night and I told the boys one they didn't know about--the time you tried to stagger out on the deck of that little tub we crossed the Atlantic in during one of the worst gales of the year (you had to see firsthand what it was really like outside). The ship was lurching violently and that breaker caught you almost by the seat of your pants while you were trying so desperately to make it back into the cabin. Pardon me for laughing, Billy, but you were the funniest sight in the world-- riding on the crest of a wave that filled the door completely, in a sitting position, with a very surprised look on your face. You tumbled all the way down to the lower deck with that torrent. I thought you'd get pneumonia, and you almost did, so it wasn't so funny after all. . . .

There was the St. Lo liberation. I'll never forget it. You ran from ditch to ditch with a notebook in your hand while the shells were popping in like ripe tomatoes. It was late that night when you got back to camp, grimy and trembling, and covered with blood. You had been pulling wounded doughboys out of that hellhole and getting them out of danger. But when you got back, you still sat down and hammered out one of the best stories of the war.

What else can I say, Billy boy? I feel all broken up inside without you around. The old zip is missing and all our grandiose plans seem to have lost their flavour. But I have a hunch you're running around upstairs as fast as your short legs can carry you raising the roof because I'm writing a letter instead of running down and finishing the story you started so well.

So I'll sign off now, Bill, as there's not much else to write.

Well, as you can imagine, I canceled my plans until I could get a hold of myself. It took a month or so. Hugh Baillie, the president of UP, asked me to come back to work for them, which I did, because that was like home and because they said they would send me over. Everyone was so wonderful to me when I came back to work. At first, it was terribly hard to see all the people who had known Bill and me as a couple. It was so hard to see the places Bill had been such a part of. I didn't relish the idea of being alone, of not having the family and home Bill and I had planned, that we had looked forward to. At times, I got very blue, and could have become quite bitter. But that would have been bad. Bill would not have liked it.

And then I suddenly realized how many friends I had. Bill and I together had had so *many* friends. They were by now all over the world. I realized I would never be in a strange and lonely place. All the world, of course, was lonely then. But I knew I'd always have Bill--no matter what--and that made living more bearable. And I remember thinking that if there was anything to the belief in another life, someday Bill and I would meet again, starting where we had left off. For that I hoped and prayed.

I got a new accreditation and finally left for Europe, thinking that it was now up to me to go on and do the things Bill and I had planned to do together--cover the war.

In November, I sailed from New York to England with many emotions--excitement, sadness, I suppose some apprehension. In London, I stayed in a huge, white, modern apartment building north of Regents Park. It was called The White House. German rockets occasionally exploded in the vicinity, although they didn't really worry me. The V-2s were much less nerve-wracking than the V-1 fly-bombs, whose whistle while in flight was quite terrifying. The V-2s gave no warning whatsoever. If you heard the blast, you knew you were okay and that there wouldn't be another one for a few more hours. The sound of the blast carried for several miles.

Right after I arrived in London, I called Henry Thompson, one of my old boyfriends from Tyler. His parents had asked me to check up on him. Henry had enlisted in the Army Air Corps, and was stationed at an airbase not far from London. He flew a P-51. We met a couple of times for dinner. And then I didn't hear from him, so I called him at the airbase. Someone answer the telephone and explained, "I'm sorry, but you can't speak to him. I don't think you can ever speak to him again."

That was an odd thing to say, I thought. Well, it turned out that Henry had been killed. He had been flying and crashed. So I had to write his parents about that.

When I reported for work at UP's London bureau, Bill Higginbotham horrified everyone by putting me in charge of the news desk. I think he'd done this more as a prank to needle the men in the office. My intention was not to stay at the London office very long, but to move on to the continent. But I did write quite a few stories while I was there. Among them was one on a tour I made of hospitals at Christmas time; one on the people who were sleeping in the London underground shelters because they were afraid of the bombs; a number of V-bomb incidents; one on American Red Cross girls in Britain. And there were others, such as what Czechoslovakia was going to do about recognizing the Polish Lublin government; what was going to happen to the Carpatho-Ukraine section of Czechoslovakia; when the Czech government was going to move back to its homeland; the Czech attitude toward the Curzon Line; and what King Peter of Yugoslavia was going to do next, and why.

I interviewed a number of people while I was stationed in London. Lady Mountbatten.[7] Sir William Beveridge.[8] Lady Astor[9]--I'd called for an interview and met her in her office. She hadn't gone into retirement yet, but told me at the time that she was planning to retire. In fact, she'd called to give me the scoop on her retirement. She liked me, and I liked her. She was quite bright. She invited me to her estate at Cliveden, and I spent the weekend of November 18 there. Cliveden was a very luxurious spot, pleasant, and somewhat strange. I found it difficult not to giggle whenever I heard her call for her husband, Waldorf. The name sounded funny. She and I went for walks together. She talked about her background and my background--nothing very reportable.

Soon after my visit to Cliveden, I left London. I had kept asking the London bureau manager when I was going to be sent over, and he had kept repeating "soon" and "relax." I was assigned to Paris first, where I stayed at the Hotel Scribe with all the other American correspondents. I remember John Phillips, Bill Walton, and Charles Wertenbaker of *Time* magazine, Acme photographer Robert Capa, *Life* photographer Ralph Morse, *Life* correspondent Will Lang, *March of Time* producer Richard de Rochemont, William Shirer of CBS, Bill Chaplin of NBC, Russell Hill of the *New York Herald Tribune*, *New Yorker* correspondent Janet Flanner--she was a terrific gal. Hank Wales of the *Chicago Tribune*. I remember the time Hank and I were driving in a jeep along a road flanked by GIs. They saw me and started waving and wolf-whistling. Hank's only comment was, "You'd think them guys never saw a jeep before."

And then there were the other women correspondents. I liked Flora Lewis very much. She was with AP. Mary Welsh wrote articles for both *Time* and *Life*. She had a noble look, was quite nice, pleasant. She was Ernest Hemingway's fourth wife. And, of course, there were Iris Carpenter of the *Boston Globe* and *London Herald* and Lee Carson of International News Service, the agency which later merged with UP to become United Press International. Because Iris, Lee, and I filed so many of our stories from inside Germany, the Army dubbed us the "Rhine Maidens." An article about the three of us entitled "The Rhine Maidens" appeared in *Newsweek* in March 1945. The writer stated that Lee, Iris, and I--" a titian-haired redhead, a Hellenic-looking blonde, and a brunette"--had press-relations officers at SHAEF[10] headquarters "in a stew." They certainly *were* in a stew, because we were doing all we could to get the big story. "The Army's Chesterfieldian view is that the presence of women up front distracts the soldier," *Newsweek* continued.   "But the three correspondents had disproved this. They asked no favors and gave none. They dug their own foxholes, and took front-line life without complaint.   But other women correspondents in Paris demanded irately, 'If they can, why can't we?'"

It's very true. Iris, Lee, and I were tenacious. You'd have to be to be there in the first place. In fact, the press corps in Paris was betting that the three of us would end up entering Berlin with the front-line troops.   We were competitors, but friends. We saw each other frequently, but didn't particularly spend a great deal of time together as a group. No, there weren't any "cat fights." We helped each other if we could without giving anything away. There was enough war around us. We didn't need our own private war. We supported each other as far as the military was concerned. If the Army was taking out after just one of us, we stuck together. We had to.

Early in the war, the Army decided that women correspondents could go no closer to the front lines than Wacs[11] or nurses. The men correspondents could go as far as they wanted.   But I repeatedly disobeyed those regulations by going out for my stories beyond the forbidden point. I was there to get a story, and I wasn't going to get it from some Paris bar.

Ann Stringer in her front line uniform, Germany, 1945.
(Allan Jackson)

In mid-February, I heard that Americans were going to jump off across the Roer.This was going to be the first major river crossing into the heart of Germany. And so I teamed up with Cliff Daniel of the *New York Times*. The two of us took a jeep to the west bank of the Roer, across from Juelich.

The winter sunshine was warm. High overhead, the snowy exhaust trails from our fighter planes unraveled through the sky in white embroidery above the smoke clouds of battle. We cowered behind a tree, waiting, not knowing where the shots might come from. Because the Germans had already blown the bridges, Cliff and I got a hold of a little rowboat and rowed across to the Citadel itself. At the time, the Americans were trying to build pontoon bridges across the Roer. The Germans high inside the Citadel could see what the doughboys were doing and were radioing the American positions to Nazi soldiers below. German mortar fire directed by radio from the Citadel kept destroying the pontoon cables as the American engineers tried to stretch them across the river.

The Citadel was a sixteenth-century fortress surrounded by a water-filled moat. Cliff and I arrived at the front gate, not knowing whether or not to go in. Three German guards were standing there. They let us in. I don't know why they did so. It didn't make any sense to us. They apparently could see that we were correspondents. We weren't causing them any problems, and weren't armed. Maybe they felt that it was simply a matter of time before the GIs took the Citadel. We told them we just wanted to come in and look around. I didn't have any problems with the Germans. I had more problems with the Americans after I came out and filed the story.

Cliff and I walked into the Citadel. It was neat, with big rooms like those in an office building. Inside its enclosure was a modernistic swimming pool which when we saw it was filled with rubble, mud, and shallow rain water. I don't recall seeing anyone inside the building. We went up the staircase, looked out a window, and saw the Americans on the opposite side of the river. There weren't any shots being fired from the Citadel while we were there, but American flame-throwers were pummeling it. That was my first day under fire. We didn't stay very long, because we were naturally uneasy about being there in the first place. We could have been bombed by our own planes.

And so Cliff and I left before the Citadel was attacked--liberated, it that's the word you want to use.

As we came out, we met a few frightened, mud-caked doughboys who had arrived to capture the Citadel. The last living Germans--four of them--had fled through the tunnels in the rear wall and were scampering over the neighboring hillside. The first GI to enter the fortress was Sgt. William Simpson of West Hartford, Connecticut. "I was plenty scared," he later told me. "We didn't know what was waiting for us inside these walls, so we just walked in slow and waited."

Cliff and I walked along the rubble-filled streets of Juelich and spotted two GIs crouching about ten feet apart with their helmeted-heads ducked and rifles pointed. As we dropped to the damp ground behind a low stone wall, the Yanks told us that a German sniper was hiding in a building about a block away. He had been taking pot-shots in their direction. Our questions were stopped by the hollow sound of a Nazi rifle. It was a defiant, lonely crack that seemed to have no echo. Then came the sharp report of a big gun, a shrill whoosh, and a deafening explosion. Two doughboys jumped up, ran crouched across the roadway, and disappeared behind a side wall.

After a few minutes, there was a series of shots, but this time they had a different ring. The hollow sounding Nazi rifle had stopped. Far off, the big gun started up again. The sound of bombardment trebled into a roar. But a new sound--different from the others--joined in. It was a searing swish, like the blast from the open door of a giant furnace. Several hundred yards to our right, vivid flames were shooting toward the same stubborn objective. The flames rushed orange and savage in a long clinging stream through the already blackened trees. For a few minutes, the flame-throwers hurled their fiery blasts and then suddenly stopped. It meant the stubborn point had given up.

Cliff and I rowed back across the river. I sent my story on with a courier, I can't remember who, but it was someone I trusted. That was often the way it was. I'd find someone reliable who would take my story and put it on the censor's desk, wherever that might be. The couriers were always on my side, feeling that the story was worth getting out. From the censor's desk, the story would be radioed to Paris, and from there to New York. The dateline on this one read 'INSIDE THE JUELICH CITADEL, GERMANY, FEB. 24, 6:30 P.M."

Of course, the Army wasn't at all happy with the dateline. But my subsequent "notoriety" made it a little difficult for them to discipline me. Several weeks after I'd written my story from "inside the Juelich Citadel," UP ran a full-page advertisement in *Editor and Publisher* featuring me.

NEWSPAPERMAN

Ann Stringer

UNITED PRESS

The U. S. 9th Army had written off Juelich as cleared of German troops. But from around corners of broken houses, from the cover of the rubble and rubbish in the dead streets, American riflemen still sighted at Nazi snipers.

Watching and taking notes on the steathly dwelling stood Ann Stringer, war correspondent of the United Press.

This young widow of a reporter killed in action in France last summer had been working ever since she got overseas several months ago for a chance to get to the front.

When she got her chance she made it brilliantly good.

Her dispatches from Juelich and Herrath and Baal—said one fellow correspondent, a man —— were "among the sharpest filed from the front by any man or woman correspondent."

The nation-wide front-paging and featuring of these and others of her recent stories confirmed her further as a newspaperman both by profession and performance.

Ann Stringer's enthusiasm, her bravery, her sure-handed skill as a reporter do credit to the entire body of United Press war correspondents. She is taking a notable part in "the world's best coverage of the world's biggest news."

It read in part, "Ann Stringer's enthusiasm, her bravery, her sure-handed skill as a reporter do credit to the entire body of United Press war correspondents. She is taking a notable part in the 'world's best coverage of the world's biggest news.'" But what really pleased me about the advertisement was the heading. Next to a photo of me in uniform was the title--in caps—"NEWSPAPERMAN ANN

29

STRINGER." Not "newspaperwoman." This was a great compliment at the time, for UP had recognized that I was doing my job as well as any man could have done it. That's what Boyd Lewis, UP's European News Manager, said at the time in a letter to my mother. "You can no doubt appreciate," he wrote, "that no finer tribute could be paid professionally than to call Ann 'newspaper*man*.'"

CHAPTER THREE

The Remagen Bridge and Dusky Devastators

Right after my story from inside the Juelich Citadel, UP assigned me to the Ninth Army Press Camp at Maastricht, Holland. It was headed by Maj. Barney Oldfield. Before I had ever met Barney, he had read my Juelich Citadel story in the Paris edition of the *Herald Tribune*. And he wasn't at all pleased with it. My story from inside the Citadel had prompted SHAEF to reissue its orders forbidding women correspondents to go no farther than "women's services" were allowed to go. Rules were rules. The "new orders" were to be brought specifically "to Ann's attention." And that's what Barney did.

At our very first meeting, he called me in and read me the riot act, chewing me out in front of all the other correspondents. I burst into tears, and ran into the ladies' room. The other reporters looked at Barney as if he were an ogre, especially when he said that if I didn't obey the rules, I'd have to leave the press camp.

Of course, it was nice at the press camp. The Army arranged for our housing. In Maastricht, most of the correspondents stayed at the Hôtel du Lévrier. The reporters always lived in a building. We were never in tents. Usually, we had a room to ourselves, heat and running water. Even when we were out on a story, we'd spend the night in a building of some sort, a hotel or private home. We weren't sleeping out under the stars.

Another advantage of the press camp was that you were close to the PX, where you could buy different things, although it didn't offer a lot of luxury items. I never had to beg for escorts when I went there, because I didn't smoke cigarettes at the time, and would always give my male companions a pack out of the carton I would get. I'd usually go to the PX with two GIs. I'll never forget one visit. The PX sold candy bars, toiletries, cigarettes--things like that. One day when I was making my regular visit with my escorts, I saw these lovely little boxes. They looked like jewelry boxes. They were small, oval-shaped, made of metal, and artistically decorated. And so I bought not one, but two of them. The man who sold them gave me a strange look, but didn't protest. My escorts also had very strange looks on their faces. After I returned to my quarters, I opened the boxes and found condoms inside.

There was a mess hall at the press camp. The weekly cost for food was a little more than five dollars. It was pleasant, but not so pleasant that I'd prefer living there to getting the story I was supposed to be getting, doing what Bill and I had wanted to do--get the big story. Despite the Army's rules, I still viewed those restrictions on women correspondents to be a violation of my accreditation as a war correspondent. Of course, reporting from the front was taking a chance. We could have been either killed or captured, although we never thought about falling into enemy hands. I don't know of any women correspondents who were ever captured by the Germans.

The main problem women correspondents had was not with the Germans or the GIs themselves--they always treated me with respect, and I don't think it was just because all correspondents carried the rank of captain. But our main difficulty was with the facilities. The men never had to worry about this. I remember many times driving along a road in a jeep with my long hair flowing from underneath my helmet and seeing GIs by the side of the road, all urinating. They were usually standing on the other side of the jeep, so you couldn't actually see them. All you could see were the waterfalls. After a while, I didn't think anything of it. It was just human. The women were even a little jealous of them, because we couldn't do that, and "using the facilities" was always such a great production.

The only facility allowed us was the general's latrine, under escort, with a guard stationed outside. The general's latrine was sacrosanct--the GIs wouldn't come barging in without checking. When Gen. Terry Allen of the Timberwolves once tried to get into his own latrine, he was stopped by the guard. The General asked the sentry why he couldn't go in, and the guard replied that if he did he'd be faced with a furious woman correspondent--me. Gen. Allen just stalked around and muttered, "Women! Women!", turned, and walked away.

By the time I arrived in Maastricht, press camp quarters at the Hôtel du Lévrier were full. And so I stayed first with Mayor Mynheer van Kesstart and his family. I later moved to the house next to the mayor's. The mayor and his family seemed to like me very much, and were awfully nice. They treated me as if I were a member of the family. One time--I don't remember exactly when--I left Maastricht to get a story, and when I returned, one of the mayor's sons ran down the street shouting in Dutch, "Ann Stringer's back in town! Ann Stringer's back in town!" Naturally, that made me feel good.

My most embarrassing memory of Maastricht was the unfortunate "shoot-out." Several hours after my blow-up with Barney, I went out for a drink with Unipresser Jimmy McGlincy, then returned to my lodgings. I was still quite upset. By the following morning, I was even more upset--I found myself in Jimmy's hotel room. But I'll let Barney tell the story:

"That night, Maj. R. A. Griffin and I had been in our beds for about an hour when McGlincy popped into my room, turned on the lights, and shook me awake. 'That Dutchman has her locked in,' he said. 'I want to get her out of there.'

"'Locked in where?'"

"'He's got her locked in his house. I brought her home tonight from the Club. She had been crying after you abused her, so I took her over there. When we came home, the Dutchman let her in, but pushed me back out in the street and slammed the door in my face.'"

"The clock on the nightstand was right at midnight."

"'After all, that's a private house,' I reminded him. 'This Dutchman probably has some ideas of propriety. He possibly thinks it's a little late to be letting you in.'"

"'Propriety hell,' said McGlincy, now pacing the floor, and he vowed he was going to get Ann out of that house. 'I'll give her my room,' he said. 'I'll sleep in the lobby.' He stormed out of the door, slamming it behind him and leaving all the lights on. Griff turned them out, and we both went back to sleep thinking it only one more of those nights. 'Women,' said Griff, as he spanked his pillow and punched it under his head."

"In the morning, I came downstairs and went to my desk where my usual fare was a pot of hot chocolate in preference to another batch of powdered eggs. Right at the foot of the steps, McGlincy was asleep in his bedroll. He looked very strange, and on closer inspection was found to have one strip of adhesive bandage going from ear to ear and another from his forehead to the back of his neck, giving him the appearance of a hairy hot-cross bun. It was hard to tell whether the furious red at the edges of the cloth was blood or some medicinal daub. A quarter hour went by and Lt. Pecor came into the lobby on the way to the dining room. He was shy a batch of front teeth. Next came Barney McQuaid, *Chicago Daily News*, one of whose hands was wrapped tightly about the knuckles. Ann came to breakfast, too, and her eyes were swollen from crying. From all appearances, it was the starter of a great day, or the aftermath of an explosive night.

"Explanations came rather quickly from all sides, but they started with none of the press corps principals. The Dutchman from the house next door came in and buttonholed 'Sydney'--Maastricht innkeeper Mynheer van Egerschot. We had nicknamed him 'Sydney' because he reminded us of the actor Sydney Greenstreet. There was a furious flurry and an accusatory waving of a finger under Sydney's nose. He beckoned for me to join him. 'My friend,' he said, 'is very upset.' His friend corroborated this by walking angrily in a small circle about the lobby. 'There have been a shooting,' said Sydney.

"Our callers now increased as two US Army military policemen walked in. It was not yet 9 a.m., and the place was jumping with lawful authority and righteous indignation. The Dutch neighbor had asked the Maastricht police to inform the American military and have them come to the hotel.

"'And who has done this shooting?' The Dutchman walked stiff-legged to the sleeping McGlincy and pointed. He then crooked his finger in invitation for us all to accompany him. Sydney got his hat and the MPs tagged along with us to the street from which the morning fog had not yet lifted. The Dutchman paused dramatically before his door and put his finger on a hole in it. He then plunged his hand in his pocket and came up with a flattened leaden pellet. Swinging open the door and leading us into the vestibule, he indicated a line around the wall, up to the ceiling, and down to the floor, undoubtedly a tracing of the course of a bullet.

"'The man who brought the woman home last night,' Sydney explained, 'he wanted to come in, but my friend does not think it right. He shut the door. The lady, he says, understands. She says good night and goes to bed.' There was more discussion to indicate that McGlincy reappeared at the door to resume his pounding. 'My friend,' said Sydney, 'he says the man comes back. My friend gets up, comes to the door to tell him to go or he will send for the police. Then he closes the door--and there is a shot, through the door and the bullet goes around this room.' The military police corroborated this, saying it matched with events as told to them by the Dutch police. Ann had left the home of the Dutchman, probably to his vast relief and in the hope of keeping peace. As McGlincy was getting his bedroll out of his bedroom so she could have it for the night, a further altercation, for no discernible reason, developed in the hotel corridor. Ann took the occasion to lock the door, separating herself from the hallway carnage, and eventually the various contestants went off to bed."

Barney added, "Ann Stringer never moved across the rear areas without causing something of a sensation. Not long after the shooting scrape, she was riding in a jeep with Frank Coniff and Hank Wales, her long hair flowing out behind. Wales was the local Duncan Hines and had the cooking delights of all the division commanders' chiefs on file, so he was steering them to the best feed bag in the vicinity when they drove past a battalion of GIs. There was a long, dragged-out wolf whistle.

"'You'd think,' said Hank in his gravel voice to Coniff, "that them guys never saw a jeep before.'"[12]

The "Maastricht shoot-out" was a sensation, all right. Yes, the whole thing was a mess. Fortunately, no one was seriously hurt. UP soon thereafter sent Jimmy back to Paris.

Of course, I was extremely embarrassed by the "shoot-out." The mayor and his family had been so nice to me. I put Jimmy's behavior down to having too many drinks. He was a good friend--he'd never shot at me. But it was an unforgettable experience, that's for certain. The incident was the inspiration for the title of Barney's book about the war, *Never a Shot in Anger*.

I didn't stay long at the Ninth Army press camp. Barney was determined to enforce SHAEF's regulations concerning women correspondents. He was doing what he was supposed to be doing, I suppose. And I was doing what I was supposed to be doing--getting the big story. SHAEF finally gave in, and stopped bothering the women correspondents about filing stories from the front. That let Barney and me off the hook. And I didn't have any more problems with the Army until 1947.

February 28 was a real breakthrough on the Rhineland front. It was Normandy all over again! Everything was moving, and moving fast. It was a razzle-dazzle race for the Rhine. The Yanks sped through the little town of Herreth, five and a half miles from Muenchen-Gladbach. They raced so fast they munched their K-Rations on the march. They didn't even stop for a cup of water to wash them down. All along the line, American command posts were on the move trying to catch up with their own troops. Even the military police weren't sure where the next post would be, what roads were safe, what towns had been cleared. One colonel told me that one of his battalions had been completely out of contact for the previous twenty-four hours. Another battalion had not been heard from since dawn.

It was the kind of an advance generals dream of. But it was an advance in war. And in war, an advance is not just a game. The doughboys bypassed burning villages a few hundred yards of the line of march without even searching them. Smoke and piles of empty shells were in ditches lining the road. Ugly splotches of blood soaked into the mud. I could see the rounder GI helmets, too. And there was that unmistakable smell of an advance--heavy, hot, and sweetish. It meant that the troops were moving so rapidly that they hadn't had time to bury the enemy dead, let alone their own. The passing doughboys would pause, perhaps to place a blanket or maybe a blood-soaked flag over their fallen comrades. But that's all they had time for. They had to keep marching, keep advancing. There could be no stopping, no slowing down.

In many places, American and German medical men were tending wounded in the same shelters. I myself came across a dank cellar being used as a hospital by both. It was full of medical men--American and German--working side by side in silence, their thoughts only on caring for their wounded. Outside, the sun was shining, but there inside that dark, cold cellar an abysmal quiet reigned. No one was talking. Some of the wounded were lying on stretchers. Over in the far, shadowed corner, one of them was all covered with a gray woolen blanket. The feet which were sticking out were crossed, but they weren't moving. And no one was looking into that corner.

In the center of the room, a Nazi medic was asleep sitting up in his chair. A dying German was at his feet. They had done everything they could for the wounded man, and were now just waiting. Off to one side, Pfc. Ralph Weston of Brownsville, Pennsylvania, was sitting on a table smoking a cigarette. He was only a little guy in a big steel helmet which completely shadowed his pale-bearded face and helped hide his weary eyes. He'd been sitting there for half an hour, not saying anything.

As he finished his cigarette, he fumbled for another, but they were all gone. I handed him a pack of four which came from the K-Rations I had eaten for lunch. I explained I didn't smoke. He reached out with a trembling hand and tried to smile, but it wasn't much of a smile. He lighted the cigarette and said, "You're the first American girl I've seen in a long time. My girl's back there. She's waiting. She's been waiting for a long, long time. We're getting married when I get back--if I get back."

Weston's words broke the hurting silence. Pvt. Lawrence Cantrell, a shy, eighteen-year-old who had just seen action for the first time, edged over and leaned against the table. "I'm from Oklahoma," he said. "My hometown is Miami. I don't have any particular girl there. Only my mother. But she's waiting, too."

He looked at Weston. They didn't say anything, didn't smile. But when I walked from the cellar into the sunshine, they were still leaning against the table, close to each other. They were not as silent. There seemed to be something warm between them now--not just the dank air from the shadowed cellar.

Not long after the jump-off across the Roer, I was reassigned from the Ninth Army to the First. My favorite division of the First was the 104th--the Timberwolves-- under the command of Gen. Terry Allen. Gen. Allen had known Bill, and had even asked me about him. It was awfully good for me to be working with the very people Bill had worked with and lived with up until the last. I even talked with the same doughboys Bill had landed with on D-Day, the GIs he had fought with from that point on. Andy Rooney, who was then a correspondent for *Stars and Stripes*, later recalled, "Bill Stringer, killed in Normandy, was replaced on the job by his wife, Ann. The rest of us in the First Army press camp didn't know how to act toward her. Ann made it easy. She just picked up and did Bill's job, often with tears in her eyes."

What preoccupied my mind at the time more than anything else was getting as close to Bill as I possibly could by working like blue blazes to make up for a little of what he had missed. I tried to do everything as nearly as he would have done it. I did feel pretty weak about making such a squawk about losing him when so many thousands of women had also lost the men they'd loved. But I wasn't noble enough to take that to heart, because it still hurt me and I couldn't get the hurt out. I couldn't cry it out, although I'd tried so many times to do so.

"WHAT HAVE YOU DONE FOR GERMANY?" That was the big Nazi sign that greeted doughboys of the Twenty-ninth Division as we entered Rheydt on March 1. The sign was typical of the Nazi propaganda of Paul Joseph Goebbels. And it was particularly ironic, since our GIs were right then in Rheydt, Goebbels's birthplace, located just south of Muench-Gladbach. The Yanks had an answer to the sign--they marched in and captured the town, probably much to the dismay of the wiry little Nazi mouthpiece.

The Americans pushed through a stinging rain and deep mud to take that rambling suburb of little businesses, butcher shops, and brick houses. But the rain and mud hadn't marred the spirit of victory drawn across their faces. The grim tenseness of battle was gone by then, and their spirits were high even through the rain and under the sounds of shell fire. Some of the doughboys had gotten a few minutes respite from the war and weather in one German house, where the command post had been set up. In one corner, tending a great coal stove, was a flaxen-haired German girl who lived in the house. She had been permitted to stay along with two of her relatives who were doing everything they could to help the Yanks. In the adjoining bedroom, Sgt. Oscar Wilkerson of Lake Charles, Louisiana, lay on the floor in front of a stove with his hands under his head.

"This is the way to fight a war," he told me. "Just take it easy. I like all this comfort and luxury. Maybe it's not so bad after all."

He didn't mention the long trudging fight to Rheydt or the heartbreaking siege during the Ardennes breakthrough.[13] It had not been so comfortable then. And he didn't mention that he would be up in the front lines again in a few hours.

Sitting alongside him holding a cup of coffee was Pfc. George Overlie of Austin, Minnesota.

"You bet," he smiled, "this is the way to fight a war."

But for George, too, this had been just a quick stop for about a half hour, then off again to the front lines.

Leaning against one of the massive twin beds, Pfc. William Manns of McKeesport, Pennsylvania, pulled out a picture of a pretty brunette. "She's Miss Dorothy Penrod," he said. "She's my girl. I think she's mighty pretty."

As we started for the door, Technical Sgt. Charles Maupin of Columbus, Georgia, who had been standing with a gun over his shoulder, stopped me and asked, "If you'll put my name in the paper, maybe my mother will see it and know I'm okay. You see, we didn't have much time to write in the last few days, and she may be worried, but I sure hope not."

Two days after entering Rheydt, I met fifteen of the bravest men in the world.

They were Americans.

They had just come back from a reconnaissance mission across the Rhine, the first men of an invading army to have breached the German Rhine since the days of the Napoleonic Wars. They had ignored death the night

41

before--a death they expected any second--to form two patrols for a crossing of the Adolf Hitler Highway Bridge. Bullets from snipers' guns had whizzed about their ears. Shrapnel from artillery bursts only a few feet away clanked around them. But they got back.

I will never forget eleven of them. I saw them lined up in an icy rain. They were muddy, bearded, grimy. It was bitter cold, yet they stood at attention as the rain streamed down their faces. They fidgeted because standing in front of them was Brig. Gen. T. D. White, commander of the Second Armored Division. The General pinned a Silver Star on each proud chest. Four members of the patrol were too battle-weary to be present at the ceremony, but they too received Silver Stars.

On the night of March 7, I entered Cologne with the Timberwolves as they battled through the debris-littered streets and choking smoke toward the heart of the city. Timberwolf patrols had first entered the city at five in the morning. As the division advanced, billows of smoke rose from both sides of the city's huge, blackened, ancient cathedral. Deserted avenues echoed to the crack of rifle fire and the bark of tank guns. In a command post at the edge of the city, a colonel pleaded with Gen. Allen, "Don't hold me up, please, General! My men can and want to go right up to the banks of the Rhine now. And we *can* do it."

I saw an occasional civilian out on the street. There were only a handful--not the 800,000 of normal times. A sobbing, middle-aged Frenchman threw his arms around the neck of a GI. He was crying with joy at being released from years of slave labor under the Nazis. An old man in a German air raid uniform walked nonchalantly into a band of Americans firing into a building containing Nazis. A colonel told him through an interpreter, "Get the hell out of here!" The interpreter explained to the old man that he'd better get his uniform off or an American might shoot him.

The old man explained that he didn't have any other clothes.

He was sent back to a prison cage.

The honor of being first into the city had gone to the Timberwolves's patrol. At 6:00 a.m. Task Force X of Maj. Gen. Maurice Rose, Third Armored Division, entered in strength. At 9:02, the 104th arrived in battalion strength. The tanks ran into a half dozen street cars. In front of them were steel rails, which the Germans had thrown up as roadblocks. One tank just plunged into the middle and drove an alley wide enough for the others to follow through. Task Force X commander Col. L. L. ("Tubby") Doan, a tall, handsome Texan, had his men put up signs reading, 'YOU ARE ENTERING COLOGNE THROUGH THE COURTESY OF TASK FORCE X.'

"Thought I'd let people know that the boys of this outfit paved the way," he explained. "Matter of fact, we've been first in a good many places." One of them had been the Siegfried Line.[14]

Two battalions of the 104th had raced to see which one would be the first infantry outfit into Cologne. Col. Gerald C. Kelleher of Albany, New York, was the winning commander. He collected a steak dinner and case of beer from the loser, Maj. Hugh Carey of New York City. Incidentally, years after the war Maj. Carey became governor of the state.

Soon after entering Cologne with the Timberwolves, I heard rumors that we were moving toward the Remagen Bridge, which crossed the Rhine. It seemed obvious to me that we were heading there. We knew the bridge was still standing. So I decided to go.

On the morning of March 10, my jeep driver took me to the west end of the bridge. At that time, the Germans were still firing everything they had, including ack-ack guns, into this little stretch of the beautiful Rhine. I didn't know when I got there that the bridge had already been mined, but I knew it was dangerous. The driver refused to drive across, and for good reason, because it was pretty hot. So I got out and walked across. My only protection was my helmet, which I generally didn't like to wear--it gave me headaches.

The shellfire was brisk. I walked across the bridge upright, not crouched. There was nothing like the almost naked feeling I had when I realized exactly where I was. I suppose I was a perfect target, but I didn't get hit. I crossed the bridge quite simply because I wanted to touch the other side, thereby making me the first Allied correspondent to reach the east bank of the Rhine. When I touched it, I turned around and walked back. The driver was amazed I had done it. Unipresser Gene Gillette was there at the time, and later said that when he saw me walking across the bridge he nearly fainted, because it was still under heavy enemy barrage.

Seeing me return to the west bank, the driver decided it was safe enough to drive across, and that's what we did. The two of us were easy targets for even near-sighted Nazi artillerymen. We rode across a battered structure which would just about have made one span of the Golden Gate bridge. Directly in front of us was a steep, jutting mountain frowning down on us as though we were trespassing on sacred territory. There was a railroad tunnel there. You couldn't see into it. German artillery shells were swooshing overhead, landing much too close for comfort. The spiraling swish of our own shells was almost as terrifying. To make the picture complete, we had been warned not to drive more than five miles an hour across the bridge. We felt as big as a mountain as shells came roaring around us.

Coming off the bridge, we could see that all had not been easy for our boys. The first thing we noticed was a burning jeep and truck sending up hot flames and black smoke. They'd been hit a few minutes earlier. Then the full-throated roar of our anti-aircraft artillery opened up as a lone German plane appeared over the mountain. Glittering tracer bullets quickly pinpointed the plane from every direction. After swerving dizzily, the plane veered off. Another German fighter tried the same stunt a few seconds later, but the barrage was too much for him. Flames suddenly spouted from his plane. It went into a screaming dive, and seemed headed straight for us, like a great flaming bird. You could almost see your personal initials stamped on each of those burning wings. The plane zoomed about two hundred feet over our heads, so low we could see the frantic pilot trying to get out. But the plane crashed with the pilot still inside. Obviously, these were suicide missions. It was almost inconceivable that the pilots could have been very eager to undertake them.

The thunderous noise from what may well have been the greatest concentration of anti-aircraft guns ever assembled ripped through the Rhine valley. And then it stopped--abruptly, as if on signal from an orchestra conductor. Overhead, a spurt of flame shot out from a Lightning fighter. A burning wing spun off and the plane plunged crazily to earth. A white parachute slowly blossomed as the pilot drifted safely behind our lines. The flaming plane was an ugly sight, sending chills up and down the spines of those who had been watching from below.

That great mass of American guns was concentrated there to ward off any German plane venturing into the area of our bridges across the Rhine. Hundreds of "trigger-happy" crew men were stationed throughout the entire section, sometimes only twenty yards apart. And they blacked out the sky with the smoke from the flakbursts whenever a plane was sighted. The fire was so intense that often Nazi planes were able to hide behind the flakbursts themselves in order to escape the eager eyes of our batteries. In such a sky filled with planes and clouded with shellbursts, it was sometimes difficult to identify a plane in a split second. It was all the harder to keep the fire pinpointed on the right plane when the target was moving hundreds of miles an hour.

But the Americans were taking no chances. "We were sent here and told to guard this bridge," Pvt. Robert E. Neff of Elkhart, Indiana, told me. "And that's exactly what we're doing. Boy, I sure wouldn't trade places with those Nazis up there. They must be crazy to come over here."

It looked to me as if the Germans were facing a hopeless task in trying to contain our bridgehead. Our troops were steadily pounding farther and farther east. Supply lines to the bridgehead were carrying unbelievable quantities of materiel. Great trucks were pushing slowly toward the river in a jam-packed line, reminding you of a slowly lumbering elephant parade at a circus. The east side of the Rhine was clogged with a pile of supplies almost as great as it had been on the west side the first day of the crossing.

Some people said that my walking across the Remagen Bridge showed I had a death wish. They remarked that I always sat in the most exposed seat in a jeep. Correspondents always shared a jeep. It was assigned to two of them and their driver. I always took the back left seat, which was the most vulnerable and most uncomfortable. I took that seat because that's where Bill had been when he was hit. I just felt it was my seat. Besides, I could see more in that seat. Other correspondents consequently always thought I was a favorite partner, because they preferred to sit in the front seat, which at least had the windshield as protection.

But I didn't have a death wish. I preferred to stay alive and get the story. Bill hadn't been afraid of dangerous situations. Why should I have been?

Two days after my story from the Remagen Bridge, I rode with American troops into Bad Godesberg. That was the resort city where Prime Minister Neville Chamberlain and Hitler had met just prior to the Munich Conference in September 1938. Until we got there, Bad Godesberg had been untouched by the war. The luxurious Dreesen Hotel, where Hitler and Chamberlain had conferred, and where Hitler and Foreign Minister von Ribbentrop had stayed, was still overlooking the gray, haze-covered Rhine. But it was a far different place now from what it had been during the conference that had given birth to the phrase "peace in our time."

When American troops arrived on the outskirts of Bad Godesberg, a delegation of townspeople, led by the Swiss consul, met them on a nearby hill and requested that the artillery not shell the city, where there were fourteen hospitals. The Americans agreed, and the townspeople formally surrendered the city. Ironically, it was German troops themselves who tried to destroy Bad Godesberg, shelling it from the other side of the Rhine, where they had been driven by the advancing doughboys. The Nazis attempted to raze the town with small-arms fire, artillery, and planes.

Failure of the German armies in the Battle of the Bulge in January 1946 had marked the downfall of Marshal Karl von Rundstedt, who had then been replaced by Marshal Walter Model. That's what the hotel manager told me on March 20 in Burgbrohl. Although he had asked that I withhold his name from my story, he acknowledged he had managed the modernistic and swanky Korfurstenhof Bad Tonistein near Burgbrohl. That was the place where the Germans had planned the Ardennes offensive.

"Von Rundstedt and Model set up their Western Front headquarters here on November 5 and began planning what turned out to be the Battle of the Bulge," the manager said. "They used to work late, and at nights took long walks in the woods. On November 8, they worked throughout the night when it was thought they had completed their plans."

Model, the manager explained, had returned to the hotel after the offensive had been broken. He had then been informed of the American advance and was advised to move back immediately. But the First Army had advanced quicker than anticipated, and Model was forced to move fast. "He was having lunch when he received the call," the manager said. "He came back to the dining hall, sent orderlies to his quarters in a chateau across the road to pick up his luggage, and resumed his lunch. Within three quarters of an hour, he was en route across the Rhine. The rest of his staff moved out two days later." The manager portrayed Model as a typical Prussian general, always wearing a monocle and declining to mingle with his men.

By April 3, I was with the Timberwolves as they were passing through Scherfede, a village nestled in a pine forest. Unfortunately, Scherfede had to learn the hard way what war was. When our troops had approached it the previous evening, they'd known that SS troops were hiding there waiting for them. And so the Americans set up a loudspeaker and told the villagers in English and German that they were surrounded, that they didn't have a chance, and that they should come out and surrender. Some of the civilians did so, but the SS troops remained.

By the time of the deadline, the SS had still not left Scherfede. So the Americans turned their artillery loose on the village. Many houses crumpled into the streets and smoldered. On one street, four milk cows lay dead, their stiff legs poking straight into the air. I saw a little old woman digging in the wreckage of what had been her house looking for something from her home to take away with her. Probably she didn't know just what she was looking for--something from her home to keep. A young woman came running down a street pushing a baby buggy. In it was a little girl, about eighteen months old. She was lying in the buggy in a pink blanket, one side wet with blood.

The weeping mother pushed the buggy to an American first-aid station. The medics dressed the gaping wound in the child's leg. That's all they could do. They told her the best thing she could do was to take the baby home and call in a German doctor. Our doctors had their hands full with their own wounded.

Twenty-two captured SS men in black leather togs were marched through Scherfede. The bodies of three more SS men were on a hill outside town. And in a little valley nearby was a wounded SS guard. Through their binoculars, our doctors could see that he was lying on a grenade. They would have gone almost anywhere to help the wounded, even a Nazi. But they were not foolish enough to approach a wounded German lying on a grenade.

Teaching Scherfede about war had cost the lives of many Americans. But it had certainly cost the Germans, too.

The same day I visited Scherfede, I heard of the heroism of the "Dusky Devastators," an all-black platoon which had tangled with an SS unit. The fighting had taken place not far from Paderborn. The Dusky Devastators, seeing action for the first time, and armed with only rifles and Sten guns, had captured or killed forty crack SS troops, cleared two thickly-wooded hills, and chalked up a record to make any veteran battle group envious.

The platoon, led by Staff Sgt. Harvey Moseley of Mansfield, Ohio, had been sent in on the morning of the third to clear Nazis from two hills inside Hardahausen

Forest. They cleared the hills in record time and came back asking for more. "We'd been told there were SS men in these woods," said Pfc. Bent T. Brown of Charleston, West Virginia, a tall, slim black GI nicknamed "Big Slim." "We'd been told many times. We didn't know exactly where they were, but we found out mighty quick."

"Big Slim," the hero of the day, didn't want to talk about it. But one of his buddies started telling me the story.

"We were just making an attack across the hill," he said. "Slim and another guy were taking the right flank of our assault. And Big Slim did about one of the bravest things I ever saw. So did the other guy."

"Yessuh," broke in Slim, "that guy was a pretty brave man all right. I was walking along beside him when suddenly he shouted at me to drop. I dropped. The Germans had opened up on us and bullets were flying thick and fast. Then I saw the guy I was with was wounded. He fell down flat on his face. I started firing faster than ever then."

Slim's buddy took up the tale.

"I saw Big Slim start toward him. The wounded guy stood up--how, I'll never know. But he stood up and with his good arm started spraying the Nazis with lead, giving Big Slim cover. It was a good thing he did, too. For just about then, a German shell hit Slim's rifle and knocked the shell clip completely off. But that didn't stop Slim. He kept on going."

Here Slim took up the story.

"I reached the wounded GI and started tugging him to a ditch behind us. I pulled him out as far as I could. That's all I could do. Then both of us were pinned down again by the Nazis."

Others in the platoon came to Slim's aid and helped rescue the wounded soldier, who was in serious condition with bullet wounds in the arm, shoulder, and back.

That was just one instance of the bravery of our black troops who, seeing action for the first time, ran into desperate, trapped, crack Nazi SS troops--and licked Hitler's supermen.

Our troops by then were really having a demoralizing effect on the Germans. On April 7, I met a Nazi *Luftwaffe* flying instructor who had tucked his bride of two months into a training plane and flown from Vienna to Germany to give up to the Americans. Husband and wife had taken off the previous day from a field near Vienna and flown to Koenigswinter on the Rhine, where his parents lived.

The airman was dressed in full *Luftwaffe* uniform when I interviewed him and his twenty-year-old bride. He was twenty-three, a slightly-built, blond youth who had served in the German air force for six years. The couple had met in Vienna when he had been transferred there to train pilots. As the Russians got closer, they decided the war was over and that there was no need for him to be captured by the Russians, whom both greatly feared.

"I've been tired of the war for a long time," he told me. "The Germans have disintegrated, and the Russians are getting far too close."

They sat close to each other during the interview and seemed perfectly contented to be prisoners, as long as they were out of reach of the Russians, and out of the war. When I asked him what he thought would happen to him if the Nazis caught him, he slowly drew his finger across his throat.

CHAPTER FOUR

Death Camp

ON April 11, I met some American infantrymen who had been lost the previous night in a forest with their eighty-three German prisoners, including eighteen women soldiers who had been part of an ack-ack outfit. The doughboys' nerves weren't helped by the fact that SS units had been prowling nearby. I learned the story from Sgt. William Redman, who had led the nine-man patrol into the forest in the heart of Germany.

"We were carrying out a reconnaissance mission," he explained, "when we saw a Jerry lieutenant coming over a ridge in the woods. We captured him, and he told us that there were many German troops in the woods who wanted to surrender, but were afraid to because SS troops nearby were sending a guard over every few hours to make sure they were all remaining at their posts."

The patrol decided to go in and collect prisoners, although it was near dusk and the men were not familiar with the forest. "We walked in," Redman continued, "and the Jerries began pouring out from all sides, carrying rifles, machine guns, and bazookas which they dumped on the road. After the Germans had helped destroy the weapons, our captured officer ordered them to fall in, and we started marching down the road." The women troops, between the ages of eighteen and twenty-one, went with them. They were wearing the regular German greenish uniform with slacks, were frightened, and crying.

The platoon marched its prisoners in the direction the Yanks thought led out of the woods. "But it soon got dark," Redman said, "and we were nowhere and didn't know where to turn. We decided to stop in a little village and spend the night in a schoolhouse. Of course, the prisoners were unarmed, but it was not exactly a good feeling to know that nearly one hundred Nazis were sleeping in the room right under you when you were outnumbered ten to one, especially with SS troops only a twenty-minute walk away.

"To make matters worse, a refugee Pole came in and told us five SS men were in a house down the street, and two others were in a house right across from us. We sent the Pole to tell the Germans that hundreds of Americans were marching into the village. At the same time, we sent two of our men back to look for help. But the two got lost, and didn't get help until this morning. That left only seven of us to guard the Nazis. We barricaded ourselves in our section and felt safer. But nothing happened."

The next morning, the platoon gathered up the prisoners, marched them out of the woods--this time in the right direction--and turned them over to US guards.

War correspondents had heard of the Nordhausen concentration camp, but hadn't known quite what it was, how bad it was. I found out for myself on April 11. As far as I know, I was the first correspondent to enter the camp, which was located on the outskirts of Nordhausen. I entered the camp with the Timberwolves, who were the first to liberate it.

An estimated ten thousand German political prisoners--about half of them dead and the rest dying--were found that day in some dozen bomb-wrecked buildings in the Nordhausen camp. All the prisoners had been sentenced for "crimes against the Reich." They had resisted the Nazis, had spoken out, perhaps, against the *Gestapo*, and had declined to be fanatic followers of Adolf Hitler.

As I walked into the camp with several GIs, I spotted some little huts. They were quite simple, made of wood, maybe twelve feet by twelve feet. Small. And so we walked into one of these little huts. Inside, bodies littered the dirt floors. Bunks were stacked three levels high, with two people to a bunk. On one bunk would be a living person, and on top of him would be a dead person-- the body had already decayed, the smell was unbearable.

The living person would be too weak, too hungry to move. It was hard to distinguish the dead from the dying except that sometimes the dying moved a hand and tried to whisper a plea for food.

The GIs and I felt horror and disbelief. You were there. You could see it. You could smell it. But you still couldn't believe it. It was beyond human conception. But there it was--you couldn't deny it. We couldn't stay in the hut long because of the stench. We turned and left, then saw hundreds of shrunken bodies, stripped naked by the Nazis guards, which had been stacked like cordwood.

I was led to another stench-laden building by Pfc. Sol Laxman of New York City. Near the doorway of the great barracks-like structure was the portion of a naked body. Nearby were others. A live prisoner inside told us later that those men had been executed by German guards when they had tried to flee the building during Allied air

Bodies of inmates piled at the Nordhausen concentration camp,
April 12, 1945. (National Timberwolf Association)

raids a week or so earlier. Four half-clothed, starved
prisoners lay near the door. They were more dead than
alive.

"American!" they cried in German, holding out
skeleton hands as they wept. "American!"

Inside the barracks was another inconceivable horror.
These floors were also covered with dead and dying. Some
were still breathing. I learned that some had been in the
building for eighteen months. There were no sanitary
facilities of any kind. The prisoners had been receiving
about three ounces of bread and a bowl of grass soup daily.
Since the Allied bombings, they had been fed nothing,
although German guards had remained posted over them
until the Americans had arrived, on the morning of the
eleventh.

The prisoners at Nordhausen had been used as slave
laborers in the adjoining V-2 plant. They had been worked
for up to twelve hours a day. Many had not been let out of
the barracks for even that. Those who were still alive were
almost naked, at least from the waist up. Many were nearly
skeletons--little flesh. They had no life left in them. I

don't know how they could have possibly done any work at all, physically or mentally. They were so weak, so dazed that they didn't seem to know who we were. Most weren't in any physical condition even to speak. And you didn't want to try to interview them, because it would have been just too painful for them, and too inhumane.

Within hours after the horror plant had been discovered, Brig. Gen. Trumane Boudinot of Beverly Hills, California, commander of the armored spearhead, arranged for billets, medical treatment, and food for the prisoners. Red Cross Director Maj. Erin Prigot of New York City sent a half dozen ambulances, converted trucks and jeeps, and began the evacuation.

The V-2 plant was separated from the Nordhausen camp by a stone wall. We had known it was nearby. The plant was entirely underground--well concealed and protected, clean, and very modern. We could see V-2 rockets that had been assembled there or were in the process of being assembled. We didn't see any V-3 rockets. It had been reported as early as the first week in December that the Germans had developed the more powerful V-3, estimated to weigh from fifty to seventy tons. Nazi Minister of Munitions Albert Speer had predicted then that the *Luftwaffe* would launch the V-3 against New York by as early as the end of the month. Fortunately, time ran out for the Germans before they could do it.

The V-2 plant impressed me a great deal because it contrasted so sharply with what we had just seen. Right next to the bestiality, hunger, and unspeakable working conditions of Nordhausen was this underground rocket plant with all the modern technological advances. It was shocking to see that a people who could reach this level of technology could at the same time carry on the brutal mess of slave labor. It really was hard to comprehend.

A little more than a week after my visit to Nordhausen, I entered Leipzig with American troops. The GIs of the Second Infantry Division had been fighting their way through a pointblank flak barrage too murderous for even our tanks. For a week, the foot soldiers had been moving through the fringes of the city, fighting by night and crouching in their foxholes by day when the Nazis had made all movement impossible. They stormed and took hundreds of flak guns one by one, guns that had caused Allied airmen to call Leipzig Germany's best defended city.

The Battle of Leipzig had been much like the Battle of Brest. Giant 88-, 105-, and 128-millimeter guns had to be captured individually by GIs armed only with grenades and rifles. The area around Leipzig had been perfect tank territory--smooth, rolling, and wide open. The landscape was broken only by occasional haystacks, a clump of trees, and by Nazi flak batteries. That's what had stopped our tanks. When a flak gunner who had been trained to sight and fire accurately at a plane moving at three hundred miles an hour took aim at a clumsy, slow-moving tank, the tank was as good as gone. "It's like taking a potshot at a sitting duck," said Lt. Francis Kern of Philadelphia. "You don't even hear a shot, and then one of your tanks is knocked out."

The only way the Yanks got into Leipzig was by creeping up on the German batteries after nightfall, then knocking them out by hand, killing or capturing the gun crews. "Those ack-ack gunners were flak-happy," recalled Lt. A. J. Stuart of Nyack, New York. "They had plenty of ammunition and didn't mind using it every time they saw something move. We were just pinned to the ground every day until dark. Even then, it wasn't good, for the Jerries generally knew where we were and kept throwing in air bursts just to make sure we stayed put. And every time anyone stood up in the open, or a vehicle moved, they'd start pounding in with ack-ack guns leveled pointblank along the ground."

Crouched in a narrow, muddy alley behind a church, I watched these veteran infantrymen taking Leipzig's defenses apart, going in with rifles past their own knocked-out tanks, past the bodies of their own buddies lying along the roadside. A German shell fell near me, sending shrapnel and masonry down around my head. Knife-like splinters of steel and stone stung my hands and face. A few yards away, the body of an SS trooper in a shiny black uniform lay where he had fallen, sprawled over the sidewalk. A few hundred yards behind us, the charred body of an American was turned face-up to the sky, hanging by the knees from the turret of a wrecked Sherman tank. The tank appeared to be intact, until you looked closely and saw the burned-out interior.

A week or so after the assault on Leipzig, I visited Buchenwald.

On the afternoon of April 21, Ilse Koch, the wife of the camp commandant, invited all the reporters into her private office to show us her tattooed "art treasures" made from human skin. None of the designs was very complicated. They were quite primitive, in fact. The "Bitch of Buchenwald" displayed these with great pride, with apparently no conception of what they were made of, and certainly with no regrets or embarrassment. *We* didn't have any lampshades made of human skin, she said with pride. But *she* did! The reaction of the correspondents was absolute horror and disbelief. She wouldn't answer any of our questions, ignored them all. We were her *guests*, and had no right to ask questions!

I myself had an opportunity to examine her "art collection"--book bindings, bookmarkers, and other ornamental pieces made from skin. I touched the lampshade. It felt smooth and clung to my touch. The skin was about one-sixteenth of an inch thick. I could see the pores and the tiny, unquestionably human skin lines.

"She was a great admirer of tattoo work," explained a Dutch engineer technician who had served twelve months in the camp. "She would have prisoners with tattoo work on them line up shirtless. Then she would pick a design or mark she particularly liked. That prisoner would be executed and his skin made into an ornament."

Another "item" which apparently had been used merely as a wall ornament was an entire male chest, completely plain and undesigned. I could see clearly the nipples and naval marks, which made tiny spots in the smooth surface, somewhat like knotholes in a wood panel.

"This was not unusual," the Dutchman said. "It was just another instance of the lack of value the Nazis placed on human life. They used humans as guinea pigs in experiments on typhus treatments, on restoring sight and hearing, and in treating burns. They'd destroy the hearing of a prisoner, or put out his eye, and leave him like that for weeks. Then they'd try to restore his sight or hearing. Sometimes they failed, sometimes they succeeded, but the experiment always ended with the victim's execution."

"Sometimes," he continued, "they would put acid powder on a man's arm, letting it burn him to the bone, then experiment in treatments for it. They also experimented in sterilization. In one camp section, they kept a group of girls for these tests. They always were well-fed and well-treated and had every comfort and luxury they could want. But about one hundred of these girls died every month from the experiments."

After our interview with the "Bitch of Buchenwald," the correspondents and the Army rounded up the citizens of Buchenwald and took them through the camp so they could see for themselves what was there. That way, the townspeople could stop denying that it existed. They were "accompanied" by GIs. They naturally didn't want to come on their own. And they also didn't enjoy it. They too were infuriated and horrified when they saw what was inside. I suppose many of them had had a feeling for some time of what was going on in the camp, but hadn't really wanted to know. They were all angry at us for rounding them up and forcing them to come in, and angry at Ilse Koch for what she had done to cause it.

The last camp I visited was Dachau, although I can't recall exactly when I was there. I do remember seeing bodies still lying in the ovens. The German commandant apologized to me because he'd run out of fuel to keep the ovens running. If they'd had enough fuel, the bodies would already have been burned and I wouldn't have been "offended" by the sight, he said. It wasn't *his* fault they didn't have the fuel. It was *our* fault they'd run out!

And so I was stunned by President Reagan's visit to the Bitburg cemetery in the spring of 1985 to participate in ceremonies commemorating the fortieth anniversary of the end of the war. It was, I thought, in terribly bad taste in view of the SS graves there. I wished then that he had been with the GIs and me when we had seen with our own eyes what the SS had done--the ovens at Dachau, the tattoos of Buchenwald, those little huts at Nordhausen. After seeing all this, I had hated a lot of Germans for a long time.

Although it was terribly unjust, many of us came to hate the civilians as well. I remember one time in March 1945 when I was standing in the drive of a large German home which had been taken over for American officers. A German woman, with her daughter of about eight and son of about five, started walking toward the house, which had been their home. The American officer with whom I'd been talking approached them and shouted, "Beat it! Go on, beat it! Get outta here!"

The little boy started crying. The mother was trying to explain something, but the officer wouldn't listen, just kept repeating, "Beat it! Beat it!" Finally, the little girl stalked past, took her doll buggy from the front steps, and wheeled it to the muddy street. Her mother and brother followed.

The officer came back and apologized for the scene.

"A year ago," he said, "you wouldn't have seen a Yank doing something like that, would you? I wouldn't have permitted one of my men to do it. But after you've seen what we've seen--if you'd been through the Ardennes . . . I hate 'em, just hate 'em. Every single one of 'em--the 'cits' [slang for 'civilians'] just as much as the troops."

He spoke bitterly, gripping his fingers tightly. Yet the scene had embarrassed him.

When I recall scenes like these even now--the rotting human flesh, the dead milk cows lying on the road with their legs sticking straight out, bowls of grass soup, the baby with the wounded, bleeding leg, the girl wheeling that doll buggy down a muddy street, and the little boy crying because he had nowhere to go--I always think it is a wonder that any of us who were there came out of it with our sanity intact.

CHAPTER FIVE

"Bravo, Amerikanski!" and the City of the Dead

BY the middle of April 1945, it was obvious by the way the armies were moving that the Americans and Russians would soon be cutting Germany in half. On the afternoon of April 25, we received word of the linkup at Torgau. A patrol of the US First Army's Sixty-ninth Division had met troops of the Soviet Fifty-eighth Infantry Division. Early the next morning, the Second Division staff of the First Army made arrangements for me to fly to the site of the linkup with Allan Jackson, a photographer with International News Service. Allan and I had covered previous stories together.

The flight over the countryside northeast of Leipzig took about an hour. We flew separately in two of the Division's Piper Cubs, spotted a town from which smoke was coming, saw a jeep full of GIs, and landed in a field of clover near a large apartment house just outside of town. Allan and I got out of our planes, climbed over two roadblocks, and walked into Torgau.

Ann Stringer and International News Service
photographer Allan Jackson with Allan's
Ford V8, Germany, 1945. (Allan Jackson)

I then saw my first Russian--a young man running
down the street wearing nothing but undershorts and a gray
cap. He had a red star with hammer and sickle on his cap,
so it was pretty obvious who he was. The soldier was
dripping wet because he had just swum across the Elbe
River to greet us. At the time, the Elbe was swarming with
Russian soldiers stripped to their shorts swimming across.

When he saw the two of us, he began shouting, "*Bravo, Amerikanski!*" and "*Bravo*, Comrades!" In great excitement and instant friendship, the soldier gave me his red star. I don't know what kind of language we managed. I asked him to take me to his leaders. He said they were right across the river, which turned out to be the Elbe. I didn't know whether the village was deserted or had surrendered or what the situation was. It was a little ticklish.

He led Allan and me to the bank of the river, where we found a couple of battered racing shells. Because the bridges had been demolished by the retreating Germans, we rowed across the Elbe.

As the Russians on the east bank saw us coming, they rushed down to the river through the tall, wet grass, and began shouting greetings. Amid yells of joy and the ebullient shooting of machine guns pointed upward, we were met with cries of "*Vive*, Roosevelt!" and "*Vive*, Stalin!" (The Russians hadn't yet been told that President Roosevelt had died only a couple of weeks earlier.)

The soldiers helped us drag the racing shell onto the river bank. There was great embracing and smiles all around and patting on backs. Then all stood rigidly at attention. One by one, they stepped forward, saluted, shook hands, and stepped back into line. Then Lt. Grigori Otenchuku, a veteran of Stalingrad, came forward to make a formal speech on behalf of the Russians.

"A few months ago," he said, "German soldiers were nearly in Stalingrad. Now Russian soldiers are in Berlin, and are right here--all the way across Germany--with their American allies."

The Russians then insisted that we meet their regimental commander, Maj. Gen. Vladimir Rusakov. We started off. I noticed that almost all of our escort wore at least one brilliantly-colored medal on their greenish tunics.

We were taken to the village of Werdau, located a few miles from the east bank of the Elbe. In a building where so many celebrations were going on, I changed into my dress to look a little more respectable. I always took a dress with me wherever I went just in case I needed a change of clothes.

At the time Allan and I arrived on the scene, we were the only Allied correspondents among the Russians. However, we soon met Jack ("Beaver") Thompson of the *Chicago Tribune*, who had unaccountably been on the east bank of the river. Everyone called him "Beaver" because of his beautiful, full beard. He was a great reporter and fierce competitor, which immediately posed a big problem for me. How was I going to file my story before he filed his?

Allan and I were introduced to Maj. Gen. Rusakov, a quiet, stocky man with jet-black hair. The General was flanked by his own men as well as by GIs of the Sixty-ninth Infantry Division who were already there. We gave the Russians our autographs. They gave us theirs. The General then invited us to lunch. He told me I was the first American woman he and his troops had ever seen, and seated me at the luncheon in the place of honor to his right.

Then the toasting began!

US and Soviet soldiers who linked up at the Elbe River celebrate in Torgau, Germany April 26, 1945. (National Archives)

Women military personnel of the Red Army serve food at the linkup celebration near Torgau. (National Archives)

Ann Stringer records the conversation between Soviet officers and Colonel Charles Adams, commander of the US 273rd Regiment at Torgau, April 26, 1945.

Ann Stringer in her "emergency dress", joins her Soviet hosts in a toast near Torgau, April 26, 1945.

Toasts to victory, enduring friendship, and everlasting peace. I soon learned that when the Russians toast, it's serious business. We drank toasts in cognac. Then wine.

Then schnapps. Then vodka. Then another liquor which I couldn't quite identify, although it tasted much like grain alcohol.

The luncheon itself started with creamed sardines, then highly-seasoned meat patties. Many plates of hard-boiled eggs were passed, as well as plates of raw eggs. The Russians would break one end of the shell of the raw eggs, then suck the yolk and white out.

After the luncheon, we talked with our Russian hosts for about an hour, and had an opportunity to meet the Russian women--field nurses--who were very kind hostesses. The conversation was in German and Russian. I had a big story, perhaps the biggest since the D-Day landings, the kind of story Bill and I had always wanted, but it was worth nothing unless I could get it filed first. I knew I just *had* to head back for Paris, and quickly.

I left the Torgau festivities reluctantly and returned to the east bank of the Elbe. Allan remained behind. The Russians had to pull the racing shell up the river quite a distance because we didn't want the current to sweep us down against a wrecked bridge. Two unexploded mines were supposed to be there somewhere.

The Russians helped me into the shell and gave me a push, but the push was too hard, the shell overturned, and I went into the water. They helped me back onto the bank and into the shell. I was soaking wet, my notes were smudged, but I had the story in my head.

We crossed the Elbe, I found my pilot, and asked him if he could take me to Paris. With great patience, he explained that there was *no way* he could fly that Piper Cub to Paris, but assured me he would fly as far west as he could.

Carrying my typewriter and the film Allan had given me to file for him, I climbed aboard the small plane. We headed west. Suddenly, the pilot announced that he'd spotted a C-47 transport plane. We began following it. The C-47 unexplainably landed in a field, and we beside it.

I rushed up to two American airmen and asked if they could fly me to Paris. More than a little amused and puzzled, they asked what was all the rush. I explained that I had just met the Russians, that it was a big story, and that I simply *had* to get to Paris to file it. With much humor and no little disbelief, both smiled knowingly.

"Oh, yes," one replied. "And *I'm* Stalin, and *he's* Roosevelt!"

Sensing no point in arguing, I calmly settled on the grass beneath the wing of the C-47. In the shade, I opened my typewriter and started typing. The airmen grew puzzled, and came by to read over my shoulder. When I looked up to ask their names and hometowns to include in my story, their attitude swiftly changed.

"Hey!" they shouted. "She met the Russians! She *did* meet the Russians! Let's go!"

We climbed aboard the C-47 and headed for Paris. Landing at the nearest airfield, I still had to hitchhike my way by jeep into the city. Arriving at the Scribe Hotel, I went first to the censor's window. There I filed my story, which I had started under the wing of the C-47 and completed on the flight. I filed Allan's film as well. We both thereby gained a clear "beat" on the story of the Elbe linkup.

As you can imagine, I was greeted by differing responses on the part of my colleagues when I returned from Torgau to the Scribe Hotel. Drew Middleton of the *New York Times* came running up to me and said, "Ann, why did you come back at this time? We're about to meet the Russians! You should have stayed wherever you were."

Others said they were sad to see me back, *surprised* to see me back, because they thought I'd missed a good story.

AP ran out to see what I'd been up to--they didn't trust me. But I'd already filed the story, and there wasn't much they could do about it. They were furious. But that was that. To top it off, Boyd Lewis, head of UP at SHAEF, arranged for me to make a radio broadcast of this my *biggest* story. Gene Gillette, UP's night news manager, told me he thought my story of the linkup one of the best to come out of the European Theater.

A few years ago, someone asked Beaver Thompson about the linkup, and he said that, yes, he had been beaten to the story, but at least he'd been beaten by a good newspaperman. That's what he said--newspaperman, not newspaperwoman. I'd always thought of myself as a reporter who happened to be a woman, not a woman who happened to be a reporter. Beaver was there with me at the celebrations in Torgau, but he hadn't filed his report soon enough--he hadn't hitchhiked into Paris.

Back in the American lines, I heard a strange story that the man who had actually captured Torgau was not an American or Russian soldier, but an Irish sergeant of the British Army. It seems he had been a prisoner of the Germans there in Torgau, had escaped, and had taken possession of a bottle. After doing justice to the bottle, he'd decided to walk into Torgau and buy a gift for his wife, whom he hadn't seen for a long time. Sgt. David Colin of St. Louis, another prisoner of war, told the story:

"We prisoners had taken over control of Fort Zinna, which was Germany's largest military prison. It was located just west of Torgau. All the German guards except one had left town on Monday--two days before the linkup-- and had turned the administration of the fort over to us. This Irishman got hold of some cognac somewhere and decided to go into town and buy his wife a present. He was weaving and marching down the street. When the German civilians saw his British uniform, they figured the Allies had arrived and began putting out white flags. About that time, we saw the first American jeep roll into town. It turned out to be the lead jeep of the Sixty-ninth Division's patrol."

At that time, the Russians were still on the east bank of the Elbe, and the Americans decided to try to signal to them. "The patrol got a bed sheet from one of our prison beds," Colin said, "and painted a crude American flag on it. The Russians across the river saw it and fired colored flares. We had no flares to fire back, so the Russians opened up in our direction with artillery. For a few minutes, it was a pretty shaky time, but I guess the Russians saw the jeeps coming into town about that time because they soon stopped firing."[15] Colin told me that seventy-six German officers, including five generals, had been held in Fort Zinna, most of them because they were suspected of having been involved in the attempt on Adolf Hitler's life in July 1944.

"The Germans had been executing them at the rate of five and six daily," he said. "The last one executed was a Gen. von Davis, who had been charged with deserting to the Serbian partisans." Six of the Americans in the prison were, he said, under sentence of death, and five others were on trial for "planning treason against the Reich."

On the week of V-E Day, the office told me not to file anything, for nothing was getting printed anyway except the Japanese stuff. So Allan Jackson and I drove to Garmisch-Partenkirchen in Bavaria, and from there to the Zugspitz, the highest peak in Germany.

Ann Stringer and Allan Jackson Skiing the Zugspitz, 1945.
(Allan Jackson)

The US Tenth Mountain Division had a rest camp there, high in the snow-covered mountains. I went skiing, although I had no clothes for it. I borrowed a huge turtle-neck sweater from one of the fellows, and a pair of slacks from another. It was fun. I turned out to be a pretty good skier, although I didn't have the strength in my arms which it requires. The scenery was beautiful. From the peak, I could see Italy, Austria, Germany, and Switzerland.

At about the time of my skiing trip, I went to Berchtesgaden. I just wanted to see Hitler's "Eagle's Nest." And that's certainly what it was. For miles and miles, I drove up a treacherous, winding mountain road. It was frightening, for only a good car could make it without losing its grip and plunging backwards. The day I went up, there was fog on the peaks, and clouds had come about halfway down the mountain. Officials were not allowing cars to drive up because of the danger, but we got special permission.

The famed Eagle's Nest was smack at the top. Below it, I got into an elevator and went straight up through solid rock to the Nest itself. The elevator was curious, having been built in two sections. Hitler and his friends had ridden in the top section. The SS guards had been beneath them. When the elevator stopped and the doors opened, Adolf and his friends would get out on the top floor, the SS guards on the floor below, which led to the servants' quarters. This way, Hitler's guests never knew he was being closely guarded.

The Nest was built of concrete. By the time I was there, the house was just a shell surrounded by rubble and camouflage netting with green plastic strips. I was taken into an enormous room which was totally empty--no furniture or anything. The room had windows circling three sides, although by then the glass had been broken. This room had given the *Fuehrer* a wonderful view of his domain. I was told it had been used only for conferences and lunches. It had no living quarters, except for the servants.

By the time of my visit to Berchtesgaden, I had become a broadcaster as well as journalist. I was offered feature work by the American Broadcasting Corporation, which had formerly been the Blue Network. My assignments with ABC were rather informal. They didn't interfere with my UP reporting. When ABC had an idea, they would cable me, I would get the story, and broadcast it. If I had an idea, I would cable them, get their approval, get the story, and broadcast it. It was great fun, though I had to work on improving my voice and manner of speaking.

Several weeks after meeting the Russians and visiting Berchtesgaden, I found Bill.

It was a lovely spring day, much sunshine, the air golden. There was a light breeze. Allan Jackson drove me in a jeep from Paris. We traveled west along the slow, curving highway past the little town of Dreux. Then we continued on to the tiny farming village of Verneuil. Two roads leading into Verneuil from the west met just outside of town. We took the one to the right, drove for about five miles, then decided it wasn't the one we wanted. So we came back to the crossroads and took the other one--the right one.

It was the road Bill had been on in the jeep that day.

The countryside itself was beautiful. The hills were rounded and gentle, and little clumps of thick-leafed green trees clustered along the slopes. The trees made a lace-like fringe of the roads. There was not a sound. We saw no one. It must have been much the same when Bill had been driving there in August.

I looked for the wreckage of war beside the road, thinking I might find a burned-out jeep. But there was nothing. Nothing. The French farmers had long since cleared it away from their fields. There was no sign that war had ever passed this way. In the background, just beyond the faraway trees, I could see the steeple of the church in Verneuil. I had been told that this place in the road was where they had found Bill, at a spot where you could just see the steeple.

Allan and I drove into Verneuil, then turned to the right toward the village of Brezolles. It was not far away. There I asked a little Frenchman if an American cemetery was close by, but he said no, there wasn't. I asked him again and again. He was kind. He tried very hard to think of the cemetery I was looking for, but said there just wasn't one. He said no Americans were buried at Brezolles, only French soldiers.

And then he thought a minute, and said yes, there was a cemetery nearby for American soldiers, close to the village of St. André. So Allan and I started for St. André.

We soon came to a sign which read "U.S. MILITARY CEMETERY," and we followed it.

Large American planes buzzed overhead. An airfield was just beyond the hill, and the planes kept coming in, circling for a landing. At a bend in the road, we came upon the blinding whiteness of countless still, white crosses set in rigid rows along the flat earth. There were no trees there, no flowers or grass. Just the smoothed dirt. And to one side, there were stacks of other crosses with no lettering as yet, not yet placed in those tight rows.

I was so tired by then that I could hardly move, but opened the door of the jeep and got out. Allan stayed behind. It was difficult for me to walk, but I went up to the entrance, to the little cleared path in the center. At the time, I was the only visitor in the cemetery, although German prisoners were working there. The view from the entrance was of crosses as far as you could see. They were all identical, very simple, made of wood, painted white. The names of the dead were painted in black on them. I walked in, a little awed by the whole thing, wondering how I could possibly find his grave. I turned to the left and walked in front of the first row of crosses.

Somehow--I can't explain it--I knew exactly where I was going. It may sound incredible, but it was as if I were being pulled to his grave. Even today I can't give a logical explanation. It really was uncanny. There were no questions to be asked, no need of walking up and down rows in search of the right cross. I didn't even stop to think that this might not even be the right place. All I kept thinking was that the cemetery was not at Brezolles, as I had been told, but here at St. André.

I remembered that I had never really received official word of Bill's death, that in the past few weeks so many hundreds and thousands of people had turned up again-- alive and free. This was going through my mind as I was slowly walking along one row when I came to the center and suddenly stopped. The cross--smooth and white--read "William J. Stringer, Jr."

I couldn't move anymore. I just knelt on the ground, on the path. After several minutes, I went up to the cross. Nailed to the back was Bill's dog tag--the one I so well remembered.

I knelt on one knee and put my arms around the cross, embracing it, and remained silent.

Ann Stringer discovers Bill's grave, US military cemetery near St. André, France, spring 1945. (Allan Jackson)

I can't remember what I was thinking at the time. I was emotionally drained. But I remember the ground was a little warm. Dry. The dirt clods and pebbles were somewhat rough. They dipped gently where the cross met the ground.

I smoothed the dirt and picked up a small white rock which just fit into the cup of my hand. I kept it for a long time in remembrance, with the dirt still on it. And every time I held it, there was less dirt, and it was whiter.

Finally, a GI who was caretaker of the cemetery came up to me and said I could get some more information at the Graves Registration Office in St. André. So Allan and I drove there. They had the first and only official record I had even seen of Bill's death. The records said he had died of "abdominal and thoracic cavities" caused by "shell wounds." He had been buried on the afternoon of August 24, 1944. They thought he had died on August 10, but I knew it had been August 17.

They had found several personal effects on him. A penknife--I didn't know he even had one. Some French francs. An American twenty-five-cent piece. And some souvenir coins. The records said where he was buried. And that was all.

I returned to the cemetery and stayed until dark. The following day, I returned with Allan. He was very moved by my finding Bill, and took some pictures of me kneeling at the grave so I could send them home to my parents and to Bill's. I thought this might make them feel better, knowing that someone who had been close to him had been there at his grave. I didn't take any flowers from the cemetery. Taking flowers seemed to me such an admission that he was there and not where I wanted him to be.

There was nothing I could do. But in a way, I thought, I could still keep him alive by doing my job as a correspondent just as he would have.[16]

In the summer of 1945, UP sent me to Rome. I was a little surprised when I first learned of the assignment, as I'd never imagined myself there. But there I was, and I liked it very much. The city had a warmth and charm of its own, more so than any other city I'd ever seen. The sun was warm and bright, yet had a mellowness and softness about it that made it never unpleasant, never too hot. The buildings had a golden tone, and the stone they were built of seemed to soak up the sunshine and glow from deep within rather than harshly reflecting the rays in a glare. It was a lazy city, built low and designed to take advantage of the beauty and warmth of the Italian skies and climate.

I was living at the time with the other war correspondents in the Hotel de la Ville. My room, which I had all to myself, was on the top floor. I had a large, bright bath, a spacious closet, a little entrance hall. The room itself had a bed that in the daytime looked like a couch. There was also a desk table and some chairs. The room was comfortable and nice.

But the prize was the balcony. Two doors opened out onto it. I usually slept out there on an Army cot. From my balcony, I could see the whole of Rome, all the things I had learned about when first studying Latin back in Texas. I could looked down at the Coliseum and the dome of the Pantheon, at the great dome tower of St. Peter's in Vatican City, and the arches of the old Roman wall lining the Via Appia, the oldest road in the world.

The balcony view was breathtaking, and made me feel very humble. At night, the sky was filled with more stars than I'd ever seen in any one sky anywhere. The Big Dipper seemed almost close enough to reach up and touch. And at dawn, the color of rose glowed over the whole horizon--a clear-blue sky in between.

But sunset was the loveliest time of all. Millions and millions of swifts, swallows, and chimney sweeps would come out of hiding and literally swarm through the sky. They'd lazily circle, round and round, flapping their tiny wings so fast that they almost seemed to spin round their little bodies. Then they'd float quietly on the breeze to rest.

Every evening at about six, I could hear music from the street far below. It was the sound of a squeasy old hand organ, a homemade Italian version of a Scottish bagpipe, and a shrill-shrieking, flute-like horn. The music came from a trio of Italians, their feet wrapped in burlap shoes, their bedraggled clothing hanging in shreds. They'd walk up and down the street playing Italian tunes. They'd repeatedly play the "Beer Barrel Polka" and "South of the Border Down Mexico Way." And we'd toss them coins.

I was living well, fat and brown, browner than I'd ever been in my life. I had such a golden brown that I didn't have to worry about stockings. It looked as if I were wearing them. And I got even tanner. It was strange being reconverted to peacetime reporting. It took a lot of study, a lot of digging. I had to make contacts all over again. Gone were the days when a story was handed to you simply by taking a long, cold, miserable jeep ride to the front while being shot at. It was safer now, but took more time getting something really good.

In early June, I went to Naples, where I joined other correspondents in interviewing Martin Niemoeller, the Berlin Lutheran pastor who had been imprisoned for more than seven years for his anti-Nazi opinions. Niemoeller had been hailed throughout the war years as a martyred symbol of the "good Germans" in Hitler's Reich. He jolted all the reporters with the blunt admission that he had been ready to fight for Nazi Germany when he volunteered in 1939 to resume his World War I role as a U-boat commander. "If there's a war," he said, "a German man does not ask the question whether the war is just or unjust, whether the aim is this or that, but feels instinctively he is bound to serve in some way. I was a naval officer for ten years. My elder sons had been called up. I couldn't bear the thought that my sons might be dying while I was doing nothing."

Then the man who willingly went to jail rather than stop condemning Nazism from his pulpit tossed another verbal bombshell into the press conference. "The democratic form of government suitable to govern the German people has not as yet been discovered."

He then launched into a forthright discussion of the reasons for the Germans' acceptance of Nazism, and expressed the belief that there was little prospect of a workable democratic government for Germany in the near future. He said he personally was like the majority of the German people in that he wanted nothing to do with politics and was perfectly content to be led. "The German people long for authority," he stated. "That was one of the reasons Hitler was so successful. They have very few gifts or instincts to govern themselves in democratic fashion. Maybe they can, but they do not like to."

The plain-spoken pastor said frankly that he did not think the Germans felt betrayed by Nazism or had learned any lessons from its horrors. Questioned about the bestiality uncovered in the concentration camps, he insisted he had had no idea they were being committed. "I was shocked and shattered when I saw the pictures and heard of the extent of these crimes."

I interviewed Kurt von Schussnigg on the Isle of Capri three days after the meeting with Niemoeller. Schussnigg had been the Austrian chancellor who had so angered Hitler, and whom the Germans had eventually imprisoned. On June 8, I found the white-haired, deeply-suntanned Austrian window-shopping with his four-year-old daughter Cissy on a winding street of that story-book island. He was wearing a bright blue suit, a white shirt open at the throat, and rope-soled shoes. Cissy was a shy, flaxen-haired girl dressed in a blue, printed, and full-skirted frock with baggy blue pants showing underneath. She was holding his hand.

Schussnigg had just come from the beach, where a US Army jeep daily took him, his wife, and Cissy to swim in one of the world's most beautiful settings. Our interview was partly in an office in the Hotel Paradiso. I was the first correspondent to interview him since his liberation.

"On the afternoon of March 1, 1938," he said, "Hermann Goering told me on the telephone that German soldiers would march into Austria within two hours unless I resigned. I pleaded for a little time. He finally agreed, warning that my resignation was the only thing which could save Austria. At midnight that night I resigned. What else could I do? I ask you to remember first of all that I am an Austrian. So I resigned. The next morning when I awoke, SS troopers had surrounded my home. I was a prisoner--and German soldiers were marching into Austria."

Such was the story of Nazi betrayal which Schussnigg told me. He was not treated as badly in German concentration camps as first reported. He said he never once was questioned about his politics and never brought to trial, although the Nazis had told him several times he would be tried. "I was not allowed to see my bride until 1939," he said, "when I was permitted to have five minutes with her every Friday in the company of a *Gestapo* guard. In December 1941, they let us live together, and we had our own little barbed wire-encircled blockhouse inside the prison camp walls."

In December 1941, Schussnigg and his wife had been taken to Sachsenhausen, then to Dachau, where Cissy was born. "We had a very good time at Dachau," he said, smiling. "It was good there for us. There for the first time in seven years I was permitted to converse with someone besides my wife. We had many conversations there. I met a man who became a very good friend of mine. He was Monsieur Leon Blum, former premier of France."

From Dachau, the Schussnigg family had been taken along with 160 special prisoners to Innsbruck. Soon thereafter they were moved to a camp near Villa Bassa, Italy, where they were freed by Italian partisans. Then Schussnigg, his wife, and daughter were brought to Capri, where he was completely free to move about as he pleased. GI jeeps would take him wherever he wanted to go.

He refused to comment on his political future or that of Austria. "I am convinced," he said, "that the great majority of Germans hated the war. I am convinced they had no other choice. I believe the war was caused through Hitler, and Hitler alone."

Not long after my interview with Schussnigg, I went on a fast junket through the Mideast with a group of correspondents. We took off from the Rome airport early one morning in a C-47 and headed south, flying directly over Sicily and the sparkling blue Mediterranean until we saw the coast of Africa and the hot, burning, endless wastes of sand. We landed at Benghazi for lunch. The heat and flies made me ill and dizzy. Then we took off again and flew eastward, following the coast.

Below us was nothing but scars of dried-up river beds and rolling hills of hot sand. We flew over Tobruk, where British and Polish troops--in a fanatic and almost hopeless stand--had in the darkest days of the war finally turned back Rommel before the "Desert Fox" had nipped off the vital Suez Canal. There was nothing left of Tobruk when we saw it, absolutely nothing. We flew low and saw the crumbling walls of a half dozen houses and the almost covered-over foxholes where the foot soldiers had lived and fought and died. But that was all. No buildings, not even any ruins. No homes. No people living there any longer. Not even a dog wandering among the sandwalls.

We kept flying until we suddenly spotted the Nile. It looked small and slow. And just before catching our first glimpse of Cairo, we saw the pyramids jutting up far away on the horizon to our right. We landed in Egypt.

In Cairo, we stayed at the famous Shepheard's Hotel. In the lobby, there were great pillowed chairs, couches arranged all around the room. Egyptians in their loose, baggy trousers, open-toed sandals, brilliantly-colored sashes, and beautifully-wound turbans were sitting on the couches smoking their long pipes, sipping their drinks, and talking. They sat cross-legged, in the style of the sultans. Their beards were heavy, curly, and black. We felt very much out of place in our military uniforms in that great domed room with its stained glass, fairly-like grillwork, and mass of upholstery. Outside, on the great porch, Egyptian noblemen were sitting around tables having their afternoon cocktails. They were dressed in richly-brocaded robes of every color which flowed loosely around their ankles and from their arms. One of them was the prince, the others his high court. They had just come from a meeting with the British minister.

Cairo itself was a beautiful city, one which had not experienced the war. There seemed to be plenty of everything there. The streets were clogged with honking, squeaking automobiles and horse-drawn chariots. The natives were walking in their flowing, nightgown-like clothing. It seemed a slow, rich, luxurious life, a wonderland, almost fairy world. Yet we saw many in the city who were wretchedly poor, begging in the streets, the flies crawling over them, into their eyes and mouths. The beggars didn't even bother to brush the flies away.

The next day, we got up early and drove to the pyramids. The road was lined with little groups of mud houses, some of them several hundred years old. The natives were tending their water buffaloes and goats. Finally, we saw the pyramids, driving high up a slope, and getting out at the base of the largest one. We walked over tombs belonging to members of the pharaohs' court, walked through the catacombs, climbed a steep incline, and stood at the feet of the Sphinx.

The Sphinx astonished me more than anything else. It sat there so solidly, looking straight ahead with what seemed a look of pity. It rested its head on the sandbags the Egyptians had placed under its chin to protect it from shellfire. There it sat with its huge paws stretched out before me. I walked between those paws realizing how little I really was, and how little I really knew.

We drove through the City of the Dead. It was a real city, with hundreds of houses, mosques, and little walled-off settlements. Inside the walls were the tombs of the dead, all buried above ground, sitting upright. Their tombs looked like little stone boxes. Once a year, thousands of people from Cairo came here--for a week--and moved into the houses. They celebrated mass and prayed for the dead. For the rest of the year, the "city's" thousands of houses were locked and barricaded against thieves.

We saw the Nile in the moonlight. It was such a filthy river that if your boat should have overturned and thrown you into its waters, you had to rush immediately to the doctor and take a series of shots for all the deadly diseases it carried. They said--it was supposed to be true--that to fall into the Nile for only a second meant certain death unless you took the serums right away.

Having stayed in Cairo a few days, we flew to Palestine, landing near Tel-Aviv, then driving on to Jerusalem. That drive of about an hour along the winding, dust-laden roads of ancient Palestine was most interesting. The countryside was barren, hot, and scorched. The natives with their small donkeys--about the size of large German shepherds--were trudging along the roads. The donkeys carried heavy loads which in Texas we would have hesitated heaping on a large dray horse. The animals walked slowly on their spindly little legs. Sometimes they carried so much hay that they actually resembled moving haystacks. I could just barely see their legs and big, flopping ears sticking out from underneath.

The villages that nestled in the hills all looked deserted. I saw a person in only one of these settlements. The sun-dried brick of the houses seemed to crumble. The only vegetation was the gnarled olive trees already centuries old, little bushy trees with dust-colored, olive-green leaves. The olive tree requires little care, and is able to grow in the rocky, starved soil of the region.

Perhaps the villages were deserted because we were traveling at winnowing time, when the natives were gathering their grain into great stacks along the road. The men, women, and children would then trample these stacks to separate the grain from the stalks. Great clouds of choking dust arose from the stacks, clouds that could be seen for miles and miles. After stamping the stacks barefoot for hours on end, the natives stooped, lifted the grain, then threw it high in the air. The gentle, hot wind blew the chaff away as the grain fell to the ground. It all happened as it had in the days of the Bible. Nothing had really changed.

Then we reached Jerusalem, a fairly large city with many modern stores. Countless people there wore American-style clothes, but the old custom of wearing the scarf over the head and the draped headdress was still evident. We walked to the crest of the Mount of Olives, and saw the entire city--the Old City, its Wailing Wall, the square of the temple where Abraham prepared to sacrifice his son Isaac. We saw Mount Sinai, the Garden of

Gethsemane, the place where Christ was supposed to have been crucified, and the river Jordan.

Bethlehem was a smaller town, dirty, dusty, and hot. There we visited the Church of the Nativity, said to have been built on the very spot where Christ was born. The site was revered for generations until the church itself was built there. Beneath it were about three levels of tunnels. In one of these was said to be the place where the old stable was. To one side, there was a little altar, the floor inlaid with a single gold star, and overhead swinging lanterns with burning candles. Here, it was believed, was where the manger itself once was.

As we stood there and prayed, we could hear chanting, the prayers of Franciscan friars entering the church. We were able to stay as the friars--dressed in black robes--filed into the room, knelt, sang their hymns, and prayed.

We returned to Tel-Aviv, and continued our flight to Turkey. On the way, we buzzed the Dead Sea, flying its entire length at about six to eight feet above the water. We flew across Syria, the island of Cyprus, and landed at Ankara. On our way over the Dodecanese and the barren bleak mountains of Turkey, we had been pursued by a Turkish fighter plane flying on our tail with its guns trained on us. The Turks were very suspicious. Had we veered from our charted course the tiniest bit, the Turkish pilot no doubt would have fired. In fact, before even getting permission to enter Turkey, we had been told that we would have to fly a carefully prescribed course. The Turkish anti-aircraft batteries along our route had been forewarned that we were going to be flying over their location on a certain day. They were told that we were a friendly plane, and that they therefore should withhold fire. This was the first time the Turkish government had allowed an unscheduled plane to fly over its territory on such a junket.

Istanbul was a colorful city, our own hotel overlooking the incredibly beautiful Bosporous. We went boating down it, admiring the ancient houses with their fine mesh-like, lattice-work shutters covering the windows. The shutters had been placed there during the time of the harems so that the women could look out, but no one could look in.

We were trailed and questioned by the Turkish secret police the entire time we were in the city. However, they were not very clever when trailing us. We could always spot them. But they gave us no real trouble. Every night while we were at dinner they would come join us at our table and join in the conversation. They were always pleasant, interesting, so we didn't really mind them being there. But they must have been puzzled by some of the things we did, especially some of the tales we told.

They were so obvious in their spying that we finally decided to give them something to spy on. So one night-- about two-thirty in the morning--a few of us got up, dressed, and left the hotel just for a walk. The city was interesting, and we really did want to see it. But we took this walk primarily to mystify the secret police. We succeeded.

As we were returning from our walk, a car suddenly pulled up beside us. In it was a Turkish government official we'd met at a tea party the previous afternoon. He leaned out the car window and in a friendly manner said that he was just on his way home from a party at a friend's house. "What in the world are you doing roaming the streets at this hour of the night?" he asked, then offered to drive us back to the hotel. We took him up on it.

One night at our table we really gave a Turkish spy something to spy on. We admitted to him that we were flying around the world in a Russian plane--the largest one ever built. The Turks feared and hated the Russians so much that this statement made him almost apoplectic. That jolted him, as well as our "confession" that nearly all of us were born in Russia and had served in various branches of the Russian army or Soviet secret police. The spy furiously took notes, asking so many questions that he finally excused himself from the table, leaving before we'd finished dinner.

We left Istanbul and headed back to Italy, flying again over Cyprus, the Mediterranean, and this time Greece and ancient Athens. But there was still another thrill in store for us--we flew over and actually into Mount Vesuvius. We flew so low over the great yawning cone of the volcano--dipping one wing vertically over the chasm--that I almost had the feeling of going inside it. I was amazed to see how it really looked--like a great excavation, maybe forty feet deep and partially filled with soft, silk-like sand. There was no great bottomless pit, no flames, rumblings, or smoke. It was just a shallow cone, half-filled with sand.

Yes, I'd done many things and seen so many places I'd never dreamed of ever seeing. But the more I went, the more I saw, the emptier it all seemed. Yet when I thought of how few people had the chances I had, I began to feel that no matter what, I had to go on, that I owed it to Bill to do the things he had so wanted to accomplish. I had to keep going on--somehow, possibly by myself. There was so much wrong with the world, I thought, so few people who genuinely cared about it. I felt I had to keep trying, to keep learning, so that some day I could really help make the world a better place.

Quite frankly, I had enjoyed being a war correspondent. I wouldn't have missed it or traded it for anything on earth. It had done me more good than anything else. The work had been hard. I'll never try to make it seem easy, for war's not pretty. War made other misfortunes seem easy by comparison.

But after my trip to the Mideast, I realized I wanted no more of combat.

CHAPTER SIX

The Pope, Nijinsky, and Groza's Hands

ON July 13, 1945, I interviewed Frau Margarete Himmler, the widow of the dreaded *Gestapo* chief, on the outskirts of Rome in a luxurious villa owned by a former movie magnate.   I had to get special permission to interview her.   She was staying there with her fifteen-year-old daughter Gudrun.   I can't remember if Frau Himmler actually agreed to the interview.   At the time, she was under British custody, and the British may have arranged it.

She didn't greet me when I walked into the room, but acted as if I were intruding on her privacy.   She was a very cold woman, very detached, with an air of superiority.   When I told her that her husband Heinrich had been captured and had died from his own dose of poison, she showed no emotion whatsoever, only sat there, hands folded in her lap, merely shrugging her shoulders.   She showed no surprise or even interest when I told her that Himmler had been buried in an unmarked grave.   Hers was the coldest exhibition of human feeling I had ever witnessed.

I asked her if she was aware of her husband's activities as *Gestapo* chief. She replied, "Of course." I then asked if she knew what the world had thought of him.

"I know that before the war many people thought highly of him," she replied.

I asked if she realized that Himmler was probably the most despised man in the world after the European war had gotten well underway. Shrugging, she said, "Maybe so. He was a policeman, and policemen are not liked by anyone."

She denied the possibility that her husband could have been considered war criminal Number One.

"How could that be?" she asked, "when Hitler was *Fuehrer*?"

When I asked her if she was proud of her husband, she answered, "Of course I was proud of him. In Germany, wives would not even be asked such a question."

When I pressed her as to whether or not she was still proud of him after he had sentenced millions of innocent people to death by torture, gassing, or starvation, Frau Margarete replied noncommittally, "Perhaps. Perhaps not. It all depends."

I'd finally had enough of Frau Margarete. She sort of waved me out of the room, and I left. I wasn't getting a story from her. I was getting a story about the way she behaved.

But Frau Himmler was not the only wife of a former high-ranking Nazi official I met. I remember talking briefly with Frau Joachim von Ribbentrop, wife of the German Foreign Minister who was executed after being found guilty at the Nuremberg Trials. I can't recall precisely where it was, but I was passing her on a street somewhere, stopped her, and tried to ask some questions. But she didn't care to talk. All I recall is that she was still raving about what beautiful big blue eyes Hitler had. The interview was short.

A week after I interviewed Frau Himmler, I got the inside story on Mussolini's role in the assassination of Italian Socialist leader Giacomo Mateotti in 1924. The actual assassin, Amerigo Dumini, had been arrested two days earlier in Piacenza. My source was a well-informed American government official, who told me, "Mussolini knew he had to get rid of Mateotti if his plans as fascist dictator were to succeed. He sent to Milan for Dumini-- who at that time was a well-known thug--and three companions. Mussolini himself offered them the equivalent of approximately eight thousand dollars to knock off Mateotti.

"For a week they shadowed him. They learned his schedule, his routine, and then picked him up on the night of the murder as he was leaving his home en route to making a public speech. They threw him into a car and immediately started off. One of the thugs was injured because the car left too fast and he was dragged along. The trio had the murder carefully planned, even to the point of carrying sacks of lime in the car. They intended to use the lime to completely destroy the evidence.

"But Mateotti put up such a bitter struggle that they were forced to stab him sooner than they had planned. There was so much blood in the car, and it began dripping so fast, that they got frightened and dumped the body. They buried it in a shallow grave. Then, still scared, they decided on the bold course of driving their car directly into the courtyard of the government palace where *Il Duce* had his offices. They left it there--parked under the very nose of the police--while Dumini cleaned away the blood."

The government official continued, "The car stood outside the palace even as Signora Mateotti was kneeling in front of the *Duce*'s desk pleading for her husband's life.

The *Duce* sat there holding the blood-soaked envelope containing Mateotti's private papers, rings, and watch. He promised her that he had already given a personal order for her husband's release. Dumini himself was arrested, given a mock trial, and sentenced to five years, but was soon released. Thereafter, he was involved in a number of robberies and murders. But he always told the police that he was a special person, that Mussolini was obliged to order his release."

On June 29, I interviewed Pope Pius XII. I had requested the meeting through proper channels. At the last minute, I realized I couldn't go to interview the Pope with my head uncovered, but I couldn't find anything appropriate to wear.

So I called the maids at my hotel, the Hotel de la Ville, and tried to borrow a scarf or something. No luck. And that's when I thought of my lace panties. I had a pair of black lace panties. And so I put the panties on my head, rippled them around, and pinned them to my hair so that the lace was in pleats, giving it a more finished look. They didn't appear to be panties at all. I remember arriving at St. Peter's, running up the front steps, all the while hoping that my panties wouldn't fall off!

While I was standing outside the Pope's office waiting for him to call me in, boys--flunkies, I suppose--were coming by begging cigarettes from me. As I've already said, I didn't smoke at the time, so I didn't have any cigarettes to offer. Fortunately, they didn't ask me where I'd found my beautiful hat.

I was finally escorted into the Pope's office by one of the Swiss guards. Someone later told me that I had been the first woman who was not a maid or cleaning woman admitted to the Pope's office.

The Pope didn't meet me at the door, but remained seated at the head of a long table. He then pointed to a seat for me beside him, just around the corner of the table. He extended his hand for me to kiss his ring. But I just shook it--giving it a gentle tug--and sat back down. The questioning was about even. It was he who started interviewing me, and I was polite enough to let it go for a while. He asked me about my background and where I'd been. And then I tried to take over. I was being interviewed by the Pope, which wasn't why I was there. I started asking the questions.

The Pope showed a lively interest in world affairs, especially in the United Nations Conference, which had convened in San Francisco on April 25. He was quite satisfied with the progress of the Conference, and said he sincerely hoped that the nations of the world would resolve their differences by peaceful means rather than from "trenches and tanks."

He also spoke of the Russians. At that time, there were no diplomatic relations between the Vatican and Moscow. The Russians were then trying to get the Holy See out of Italy, feeling that it had served its purpose. If the Pope were not in Italy, his influence over the Italians would, of course, be much diminished. Well, the Pope naturally didn't go for that idea. But when I asked him about the prospect of establishing diplomatic relations between the Holy See and the Kremlin, he said in a general sort of way that the Vatican believed in maintaining diplomatic relations with all countries.

I then asked him about the Polish Corps. I had done a number of stories on the Poles, and felt great sympathy for them. Yet there seemed to be little public interest in their plight, which I thought most tragic. There were 300,000 of them. They had left their homeland and fought for the Allies in some of the toughest battles in the Mediterranean Theater, including Tobruk, Monte Cassino, and the Gothic Line in northern Italy. But when the war was over,

America and Britain seemed to have simply shaken the Poles' hands and said, "It was so nice to have known you. Sorry we've got to leave now."

But the Poles had nowhere to go. Nearly ninety-five percent of the troops and all of the 5,500 women serving with them had once been prisoners in Russia and Siberia. They had been "captured" or deported when Russia invaded Poland in 1939. After escaping from Russia-- where they had been treated as badly as the Nazis had treated their own prisoners--the Poles had fought the Germans. But their hatred of the Russians had not diminished.

And so now the Poles were literally stranded near the Italian village of Ancona, on the Adriatic. They felt that they could not return to Poland, by then completely dominated by the Russians, because they would have ended up arrested and sent back to slave labor camps--building railroads, chopping trees. It just made my blood boil. The question was not that the Poles were anti-Soviet, but that they were individuals--nearly all of them highly educated, highly talented--who were being forced by their "friends" to go underground and become homeless wanderers without a country, jobs, or friends. I thought something should be done about it. And so I asked the Pope about the future of about the Polish Corps, and he expressed a deep interest in them and sympathy for their cause.

When he thought he had said enough, he again extended his hand for me to kiss his ring. I again shook it. He rose, then I rose and left. The interview had lasted about twenty minutes.

Donna Rachele Mussolini was a lovely lady, a simple woman. More than a week after my interview with the Pope, I found the *Duce*'s widow inside the barbed-wire enclosure of the Terni internment camp near Rome. She was being held in protective custody with her two younger children, Romano, seventeen, and Ann Marie, sixteen. The camp was an abandoned synthetic rubber factory.

Donna Rachele was attractive at fifty-six years. She was wearing her ash-gray hair bound up in a light-blue printed silk kerchief. She had startlingly large, blue eyes, pretty against a pale, transparent skin.

"We were happiest in the old days," she said of her life with Mussolini. "We never really had a home after 1925. We were happy before that. We should have gone to America when we first got married. We planned to do it and talked much about it. We planned to live there and raise children there. But then Mussolini"--she never called him Benito—"changed his mind. He felt himself too powerful, and his friends persuaded him to betray his workers. But his sympathies were always with the working class."

At times choking with sobs or screaming denunciations of her husband's mistresses, Donna Rachele told me about the last days before he was executed on April 28 by Italian partisans.

"I saw Mussolini about eight days before he was killed," she said. "I talked to him on the phone about six or seven hours before he died. He called me at three a.m. and told me to turn myself and the children over to American authorities."

I asked her about the brunette Clara Petacci, Mussolini's mistress, who died with him. Her eyes flashed, she pushed herself far back in her chair, sat upright, and declared, "They would have done well to *hang* her! *She* was the only one around Mussolini who really had anything to do with the Germans."

Pounding her fist on the table, she shrilly exclaimed, "Mussolini *never* had anything to do with women! He *never* let them have any influence over him! That was just propaganda to ruin him. Mussolini would spend about five minutes with a woman. Then he would leave them. He only saw Petacci once at Lake Como while we were staying there toward the last."

I asked her whether she herself had had any influence over her husband. She laughed almost gaily, shrugged, and replied, "Of course, in a way. He really trusted me. He was very sincere. He had a lot of affection for me. Probably I am the only woman who really thought something of him. I was the only woman he ever thought anything of. He really did like his family--to an extent that no other man in the world could."

She started sobbing again, pressing her hand--with its stubby fingers and kitchen-worn fingernails--to her forehead.

"But I was never close to him," she wailed. "I was always with him when he was down."

I asked her about Mussolini signing the Axis Pact.

"Everybody is to blame for that," she shouted passionately, "everybody from Badoglio up to the King himself. They *all* blame Mussolini. *They* killed him, while Badoglio's mistress lives in Switzerland with millions of dollars!" (Marshal Pietro Badoglio, the former chief of the Italian general staff, became premier after Mussolini's fall from power in July 1943.)

As the interview ended, Donna Rachele smiled, shook my hand, walked out the door, and--stopping short--turned to me.

"Mussolini was a very intelligent man," she said. "Probably one day you'll realize that!"

She turned again, continued walking, wheeled, then shouted even louder, "And tell *them* I said so!"

Donna Rachele's eldest daughter, Edda Ciano, told a different story of Clara Petacci's influence over Mussolini. It appeared that Mussolini was a devoted family man, depending on how many families he had. I gathered from my interview with Donna Rachele that she wasn't very close to Edda. Maybe there was jealousy involved. I don't know. I had been persistent in trying to arrange an interview with Edda, Mussolini's favorite child. To get the story, I first had to get special permission from the Italian premier. The whole thing was pretty complicated. I'd first tried to interview her in Capri. When I phoned, she sharply replied, "No!" So I hung around a day or two, couldn't get the interview, and returned to Rome.

I then learned that she had gone to Lipari Island, off the coast of Sicily. I pursued her there, flying to Palermo on a B-25, then taking a train to Messina, then taking an Italian torpedo boat to Lipari. I was persistent, all right. Edda was being held in custody by the Italian government. I called her yet again. I think by that time she thought that if I intended to follow her all over Europe, she might as well just give up. She certainly didn't expect me to. And so she gave me the first interview she'd ever granted.

She received me in her requisitioned thirty-dollar-a-month cottage on sleepy Lipari Island, where the Italian government had banished her until it could decide what, if anything, to do with her. She was very beautiful, vain and regal. During the interview, she sat on a flowered love seat beneath flower-decorated photographs of herself in younger days. The servants apparently had to replace the wilted flowers regularly with fresh ones. She was dressed in tailored blue slacks, a light-blue blouse, and blue, rope-soled shoes.

Although regarded in pre-war days as Mussolini's "evil star," Edda denied she had ever had any special political influence over him.

"I had my opinions and I was the only one who sometimes stood up to my father," she admitted, "but he never let me influence him. In minor things, he sometimes took my advice, but that was only to please me. In important matters, he never did. My mother mixed more in Italian politics than I--much more. But in international politics, I suppose she did not understand a thing. Clara Petacci carried more weight with him than anyone else."

Edda claimed that Clara was so powerful at one time that all appointments with the *Duce* had to be cleared through her personally. Clara was, Edda believed, the real dictator of Italy in the final days of fascism.

"The only real and functioning ministry at one time in 1942," she said, "was at the house of Clara Petacci."

She freely admitted her pro-Axis sentiments.

"I was pro-German in the beginning," she said. "I never denied it."

Edda stated she believed Hitler was dead "because he had always said he would kill himself if anything went wrong. He told my husband in Salzburg in 1939 that he would kill himself if the Nazis failed."

As for her husband, former Italian Foreign Minister Count Galeazzo Ciano, she said she had never forgiven her father for turning him over to a firing squad.

At 12:19 on the afternoon of July 30, 1945, American, British, and French correspondents entered Vienna in a mile-long convoy after repeated delays blamed on the Soviet occupation forces. Austrian civilians, dully carrying out their daily routines, disinterestedly waved or smiled as the convoy rolled past Russian guards into the former enemy capital. American and French correspondents had left the press camp at six-thirty in the morning in thirty-six vehicles, then driven more than one hundred miles through former Russian-occupied territory to a suburb just west of Vienna. There, a twenty-minute halt was called to await British correspondents en route from Klagenfurt. Once the British arrived, the two convoys merged and the correspondents of all three nations simultaneously entered the city limits.

I found Vienna very sad at the time. It had been physically damaged by the bombings and shellings. But what struck me more than anything else was the deadness of the people. Of course, they were starving to death, like so many millions throughout Europe. They had no energy to move about. But the city was depressing even with all things considered. I thought I'd never be able to love Vienna. It was certainly no longer the city of waltzes.

It was in Vienna that I accidentally met the dance legend Vaslav Nijinsky. In early August 1945, I was staying with other Western correspondents in the press hotel in Vienna. One day, I thought I overheard the name "Nijinsky" mentioned by one of the waiters, who was speaking in German. I asked him if he was talking about *the* Nijinsky, the famous Russian dancer. He said he was. I asked, "Why? What of him?" And the waiter replied that Nijinsky and his wife were living in the bomb-gutted Sacher Hotel--just across the street.

I rushed over there, phoned from the lobby, and spoke with Nijinsky's wife, Romola, who came down to see me. She was a little edgy about talking to me because of unfavorable interviews in the past concerning her husband's mental condition. I told her I'd always admired him from a distance, but had never actually met him. We went up to their hotel room, where I met Nijinsky himself.

The interview was, on the whole, upbeat. Nijinsky was very pleasant, not talkative. Romola did most of the talking. She said the fifty-four-year-old celebrity had last danced in 1913 in the Vienna opera house's production of *Les Sylphides* and *Spectre de la Rose*. She recounted some of the problems they had recently encountered, namely hunger--food was short.

"Listen a while," she then said, "and I will tell you this story. It is something for the fairies, an unbelievable thing.

"We were living in our little house in the woods near Urdenburg and Wienerneustadt because we felt safer from the shellfire living there than in the city. That is where we were when the Russians came. Nijinsky heard them talking in his native language. He wandered outside our house, and was suddenly speaking to them. It was the first time he had spoken a word in twenty-two years. He had been silent all this time not because he couldn't speak, but because he had no desire to do so. It was difficult at first because his voice was rusty. But the Russians brought laughter, the Russians brought vodka with them.

"Nijinsky drank until the old, wild freedom surged again within him--and his miracle legs grew restless. The Russians sat around the campfire, like gypsies, and began to dance their Cossack dances. Like a child, Nijinsky sat there watching them. Then with one breath, he leaped up before them and started dancing. These Russians from the Urals, from Siberia, from the Caucasus, squatted and stared. They knew a great one when they saw him. They shouted, screamed, and clapped their hands--and would not let him go.

"It was like old times for Nijinsky. It was like the bright days before the great darkness came. They gave him wine, they gave him vodka--he, who had never tasted liquor before. He was drunk when he returned home. Drunk, yes, but oh so happy! I had to help him undress. And the first thing he did the next morning was return to his friends. He wanted to stay with them."

Nijinsky couldn't stay with them, of course, because the Red Army did more than dance and drink vodka. And his comrades couldn't take him along.

It was a great story, and got a lot of play. One newspaper ran it on the front page under the headline

"NIJINSKY LIVES!" But I couldn't really believe that the Russian Nijinsky had *never* had a drop of liquor before, or that he hadn't spoken a *single* word in twenty-two years. I took Romola's statement to be a romantic exaggeration. What she had said about his long silence was particularly hard to believe. It seemed to me that he would have had to say *something* to her during those years, if only it had been "Another piece of toast, please" or "Heat up the coffee."

The following day, as I recall, I took both of them for a drive in my jeep. It was a beautiful day. We visited the Schonbrunn Castle, which had been the Habsburg monarchy's answer to the Palace of Versailles. Then we visited the nearby Gloriette Monument. We looked for the longest time at the magnificent scenery below. As we were leaving, Nijinsky descended the steps, sort of dancing down. I'd never seen him perform, but knew who he was. It was the closest I ever came to seeing him dance.

I met Romola and Nijinsky several times after that while I was in Vienna. I regularly brought them peanut butter sandwiches, which I smuggled out of the American mess. At first, they didn't seem to like peanut butter much, but eventually grew fond of it. So I supported them for a while on peanut butter sandwiches, which wasn't unusual for a correspondent to do. We'd usually steal food from the mess. If the Army gave us more food than we could eat-- which was often--we'd put it in a napkin or something and smuggle it out to a friend who was starving--a German civilian, generally. I preferred stealing peanut butter sandwiches because they were easy to smuggle and very nourishing.

My trip through the Balkans and Eastern Europe in late August 1945 was heartbreaking, for it was there that I saw how we were failing to get along with the Russians. It was there I saw the next war, and the way of avoiding it.

At the time, the momentum seemed too great. The next war would soon come, I thought. But I'd never admitted this in anything I'd ever written or said over the radio. I'd always kept pounding away at the belief that there *was* a way of averting a Third World War. It took such little common sense on both sides, I believed, just a little less selfishness. People at that time were inclined to see Russia as heaven on earth or just the opposite. Few seemed to have any idea that she might be something in between. And so the general view seemed to be that we should either follow humbly in Russia's footsteps or go to war with her right away and get it over with. I thought that both views were not only shameful and stupid, but that they should be stopped.

We simply *had* to get along with Russia. I thought we could. But we certainly weren't going to do so the way we were going about it right after the war. Russia would never have any respect for us if we kept giving in to her every whim, if we continued our namby-pamby attitude with conquered Germany and permitted Russia--with her clear-cut plans of taking over Germany--to do so. I thought that if we continued to sit back, smile idiotically, and let Russia with her manpower, ruthlessness, and ambitions take over Germany's tremendous productive capacity, then we would one day be faced with an enemy much too powerful for us. But if, on the other hand, we said that there was no way we could get along with Russia, then all we could really do was go bury our heads in the sand or--better yet--commit hara-kiri.

These were my thoughts as I left on a 1,500-mile jeep ride through the Balkans with Si Freidin, a correspondent with the *New York Herald Tribune*. Si had asked if he could come along. Since he was not a wire-service competitor, I was glad to have him, for I was secretly a little frightened of striking out on my own. The press camp had given me a jeep and driver. We had originally intended to drive just from Vienna to Sofia, and so we took rations for only three days. As things turned out, we didn't get back for six weeks. One story just naturally led to another.

The three of us set out one Saturday morning from Vienna without papers, passports--nothing. That was my idea. I had decided to see what I could get away with. It was so soon after the war that the borders of the Russian-occupied countries had not as yet been frozen.

We drove first to Budapest. I loved the city, although it was almost completely demolished. The Russians had fought hard for it for several weeks, finally taking it block by block. There was hardly a house or building left undamaged. But there was still something about the city which captivated me. As it edged the hills at the great bend of the Danube, it was one of the most breathtaking sights I'd ever seen.

I had been in Budapest twice before, once when I'd seen bodies still floating down the river. That had been ironic. Near Vienna, the Danube was sluggish, muddy, green, never the blue it was famous for. But it was so beautiful here in Budapest. Here it was a blue, the loveliest, clearest blue you could ever imagine. Yet I had been walking along this beautiful blue watching bodies floating down it. It truly was a terrible sight because the bodies had been decomposing for some time.

After a brief stay in Budapest, we turned southward for Yugoslavia. Our goal was Belgrade. But there we ran into trouble. When stopped by Russian troops, we had simply waved our PX ration cards. Seeing the official stamp and not reading English, the Russians had waved us on. But it was different with the Yugoslavs, who stopped us, arrested us, interrogated us, and held us incommunicado. This happened all along the way to Belgrade. The Yugoslavs were very much like the Russians. Tito[17] had the country sewn up tighter than a beanbag. Every twenty miles or so, we were detained and questioned. We were traveling strictly illegally, of course. I was talking fast in a mixture of a few Russian phrases I'd picked up, some German, and a little Italian. And countless gestures. Having been on the road for nearly forty-eight hours, we finally made it to Belgrade. Then we headed to Sofia, Bulgaria.

Because our driver by then was tired, I did the driving through the woods and mountains of Yugoslavia. The country was beautiful. We stopped beside one cornfield and ate K-Rations, then continued along the highway, which eventually dwindled to a narrow cart track. The sun began to set as we passed little villages with Yugs sitting around their campfires singing and laughing. At one point high on a mountain overlooking one of the bottomless caverns, we passed Yug troops--about 10,000 of them-- returning from maneuvers. They were winding down that narrow road, barely squeezing past the jeep, singing, shouting, and laughing. I was frightened, for we were in no position to argue with them if they decided to play a joke of some sort. But they didn't, and the three of us finally reached the Bulgarian border, driving across with no trouble.

We later learned that by then the Yugs and Russians had called a quick conference concerning us, deciding to let us go wherever we wanted. They thought this would be better--since we'd bludgeoned our way so far--to let us continue. They hoped to "win us over" rather than throw us out and thereby definitely alienate us. We learned in Sofia that our progress from Belgrade through Yugoslavia and then into Bulgaria had been monitored by telephone from roadblock to the war minister in Sofia--"Jeep number so and so with three correspondents now passing point number so and so." In their reports, they had referred to our driver as a correspondent as well. You have to remember that this was the first time since the Russian Revolution of 1917 that any Americans had at will driven overland through Russian-occupied territory. It just had never been done. And our ability to do so surprised no one more than ourselves.

In Sofia, we were at first treated with some suspicion. Then the government finally warmed up and feted us. After a week's stay, we headed for the Danube again and for Romania--Bucharest. We received a little surprise at the Danube border in the Bulgarian village of Russie (Roustchouk). The three of us were completely covered with a gray, powder-like dust. Our eyes were filled with mud where the dust had been moistened by the tears of fatigue. Our hair was matted with dust. We were a death-like gray, all caked with dust. In this condition, we drove into Russie, asked where the city hall was, and drove up to it. The building was located on the town square.

As soon as we came to a stop, a few people began drifting over to the jeep. Someone asked if we were Americans, and we said we were. Before we knew what was happening, a crowd of a thousand or more was surging around the jeep, pulling at us, laughing, trying to speak and touch us. They hauled us out and onto their shoulders. It was the first time I'd ever been carried this way. Si weighed some 230 pounds. But they carried us all over that town. It was really unbelievable

Then they carried us into a big hall where they had hastily prepared a sumptuous banquet. And imagine this if you will. We still looked like goons, covered with this horrible gray dust, wrinkled, tired, and filthy. But our hosts seated us, toasted us, and made speeches--simply because we were Americans. On it went far into the night, until I almost collapsed. They finally took us to the hotel, where I did collapse. Early the next morning, at seven o'clock, the people of Russie were back. They gave us the sightseeing tour of our lives. It was only the following day that we finally were able to leave as they escorted us down to the river ferry and bade us farewell.

Then it all began again. Word spread to the Romanian side that Americans were coming. When the ferry reached the Romanian embankment, a little band struck up what struggled to be the "Star Spangled Banner." Romanians were hurling roses and grapes onto the ferry, almost covering the jeep. Again we were hauled around like gods. A large car drove up to meet us. It was a limousine the government had sent down from Bucharest to transport us in style to the capital. So Si and I deserted the lowly jeep, left it to our driver, and continued our journey in luxury.

Bucharest was also a lovely city. When I first arrived, I turned on the radio in my hotel room. I had no prior knowledge of the Romanian language, of course, but it is a Romance language, and with my knowledge of Latin I could understand the announcer saying that there had been a "spontaneous" demonstration that day in the city, and another "spontaneous" demonstration was scheduled for the next day--that showed how spontaneous it was.

I was personally greeted by the Romanian premier, Petru Groza, who couldn't keep his hands to himself. He told me he had "noble plans" for the country, but I don't know if he was interesting in anything other than pawing people. He'd keep putting his hands on me, and I'd keep picking them up and putting them back where they belonged. He wouldn't give up, but neither would I. I won the battle. But he apparently didn't forget me. I was later told that whenever he met an American correspondent, he'd ask, "When is Ann Stringer of the United Press coming back? She had the most beautiful legs in Romania." That was Groza for you.

I also met President Gheorghe Tatarescu. At least he kept his hands to himself. He told me, "Between the democracy of the western powers and the democracy of Romania there is a great difference. Democracy is relative. Compare Romania to France, where the democratic governments last an average of six months, and to the United States, where the President has the same powers as any European dictator. Compare Romania, Hungary, Poland, Greece, and Yugoslavia--and any one who is objective must come to certain conclusions.

"Romania is the only country," he concluded, "where one will find peace and quiet consideration for the welfare of the people. It is the only country where there is justice and humanity. There is no trace of blood on the hands of the present government."

I doubted that last statement, although I didn't look at his own hands.

Because I was interested in doing some sightseeing, Groza gave me a plane and a pilot. It was a small plane, not unlike the one I'd learned to fly when I was a student at the University of Texas. From Bucharest, the two of us flew northward into Transylvania, over the beautiful Romanian countryside. The plane suddenly ran out of gas in midair, forcing us to land in a field. The pilot disappeared over the horizon, and I began wondering if he would be coming back. If he did not return, I thought, I would have to find gasoline somewhere and try flying the plane myself, hoping to remember what I'd once learned in Texas.

And then I saw him just over the horizon, rolling a big barrel of gasoline. He filled the plane's tank, and we returned to Bucharest. I didn't stay there long because I had to get away from Groza.

Si and I flew from Bucharest to Rome, where we could file our stories free of censorship. What a trip it had been!

CHAPTER SEVEN

Nuremberg

A UP story filed from Frankfurt in late November 1945 told of Eva Braun's diary found somewhere in Bavaria. It wasn't my story. I don't recall the name of the correspondent who wrote it. But I was especially interested in it because of my own interview with Mussolini's widow. The story gave some insight into the kind of life the *Fuehrer* had had with his mistress.

Apparently, Eva Braun had been so jealous of Hitler and so upset over his cold attitude toward her that she had decided to kill herself several times, but had never gone through with it. By 1935, she was already calling herself "mistress of Germany and of the world's greatest man." American intelligence agents found her diary along with some silverware, jewelry, and photo albums. Although she and Hitler were married in the Berlin bunker on April 29-- just before their suicides--their lives together had been pretty rocky. She would get depressed, writing in her diary that she wanted to kill herself, then she would make up with Hitler, then return to the diary entry and write in the margin, "Just my crazy imagination" or "baloney." In the last entry--dated May 28, 1935--she had written, "I've just sent him a letter, one that's decisive for me. If I don't get an answer before ten tonight, I'll take my twenty-five pills and lie down peacefully. Is it a sign of the terrific love of which he assures me that he hasn't spoken a kind word to me for three months? Agreed, he's been busy with political problems, but haven't things eased off? . . . I'm afraid I won't get an answer today. Dear God, please make it possible that I speak to him today: tomorrow will be too late. I've decided on thirty-five pills so as to make it dead certain this time."

In November 1945, UP assigned me to the Nuremberg Trials.

Ann Stringer takes notes during testimony at the Nuremberg Trials, 1946. Seated two seats to her right is United Press correspondent Walter Cronkite. (National Archives)

I was not the only woman correspondent reporting on the proceedings from the Bavarian city. There was Andrée Violis of *Paris Soir*. She was lovely, easy to get along with, and extremely bright. And there was *Liberty*'s Erika Mann, daughter of the German writer Thomas Mann. Our press camp was quite nice, having been the old estate of Count Faber, the pencil king, of Eberhard-Faber fame. The women correspondents were billeted in the villa on the castle grounds. The men lived in the castle itself.

On the morning of November 20, I went early to the Palace of Justice just to see what the courtroom looked like. I'll never forget the scene. The room was empty except for one lone, black GI. He was dusting and arranging chairs while singing in a beautiful voice, "Sometimes I feel like a motherless child." It was very moving.

I covered the Trials for eleven months. Those who were there no doubt have their own special memories of it, as do I. I particularly remember the motion picture presentation of November 29. The American prosecutor Thomas Dodd rose and said, "We will now show what concentration camps mean. The camps were not an end in themselves, but an integral part of the Nazi system of government. We intend to prove that each defendant knew of the camps, and that the camps were instruments by which the defendants retained power. They used the camps to prepare aggressive war."

The lights in the courtroom suddenly went out. At the same instant, lights set around the prisoners' dock rail flashed on to illuminate the twenty defendants. Reinforcements of American MPs filed silently into the room to join the while-helmeted guards already around the dock. In an almost deathlike silence, the defendants-- silhouetted in the dark courtroom by the fluorescent lamps so that their guards could watch them--stared fascinated, bowed their heads low, or mopped their faces as the show proceeded. Hjalmar Schacht, the former Nazi Finance Minister, turned his back to the screen throughout the showing. Polish Overlord Hans Frank--one of the most infamous mass-murderers in world history--became ill.

For fifty-two horror-packed minutes, a tense audience watched an American Army movie baring conditions in Nazi concentration camps. I myself thought the film was only a pale reflection of what I had personally seen at Nordhausen, Buchenwald, and Dachau--the thousands upon thousands of charred and pain-wracked bodies, and that almost unbearable sickly sweet stench.

First on the screen was Leipzig--shots of bodies burned to a crisp, of men and women mowed down by machine-gun fire as they fled barracks the Nazis had set afire. Former *Luftwaffe* chief Hermann Goering leaned forward in his seat, staring. Rudolf Hess snapped upright, betraying intelligent interest for the first time since the trials began. He whispered to Goering on his right and former Foreign Minister von Ribbentrop on his left.

The camera moved slowly over the heaps of burned bodies. War correspondents had seen them before they had been piled up--agonized fingers dug into the earth. Col. Gen. Alfred Jodl put on dark glasses. Field Marshal Wilhelm Keitel bent stiffly forward. Baron von Papen--Hitler's chancellor--lowered his head, covering his face with a handkerchief.

The film went to Nordhausen, which had been liberated by the American Third Armored and Timberwolf Divisions. It showed 2,500 bodies stacked beside a bombed building. Schacht, his owl-like glasses reflecting the light in the prisoners' dock, remained rigidly facing the audience. German civilians under the guns of American troops carried bodies to mass graves. Grand Admiral Karl Doenitz leaned heavily over the side of the dock as if he had seen all he could. Keitel removed his glasses, mopped his sweating face, and lowered his head.

Next came one of the worst of all, Buchenwald. The film showed German civilians marching past the display of lampshades, picture frames, plaques, and bookmarks made from the skin of murdered men. This was the same "art collection" the Bitch of Buchenwald had shown us correspondents. Hess was still watching, transfixed. Jew-hater Julius Streicher, editor of *Der Stuermer*, stared with a deadpan expression. Ribbentrop still had his eyes to the floor.

Then came Mauthausen, notorious Dachau, and Belsen, where bodies were piled so high it took British bulldozers to push them into mass graves. And then the film ended.

The lights came on. For the longest time, it seemed, the entire audience just sat there as if hypnotized. Goering did not take his eyes from the screen until court adjourned a minute later. Schacht stood up, his lawyer stating that his client had nothing to do with the camps. He said, in fact, that Schacht would tell the court that he himself had been imprisoned for seven months in Dachau.

On December 5, the British prosecutor, Sir Harley Shawcross, told the military tribunal that the world had already outlawed aggression before Adolf Hitler rose to power, and that the twenty "wretched men" in the dock had put their heads into the hangman's noose when they led Germany into the war. Shawcross invoked the Pact of Paris--the 1928 Kellogg-Briand Pact outlawing aggressive war--as the cornerstone of international law. "The Pact of Paris," he said, "is the law of nations. This tribunal will enforce it."

Shawcross specifically named seven defendants as among the "murderers, robbers, blackmailers, and gangsters" who had led Germany into the war--Goering, von Ribbentrop, Baron Constantin von Neurath, von Papen, Keitel, Raeder, and Jodl. Shawcross stated, "In criminal courts where men are tried for breaches of municipal laws, it not infrequently happens that of the gang indicted together in the dock one has a mastermind, the leading personality. But it is no excuse for a common thief to say, 'I stole because I was told to steal,' or for a murderer to plead, 'I killed because I was asked to kill.' These men are in no different position, for it was nations they sought to rob, whole peoples they tried to kill."

A week after this scene took place, the courtroom witnessed an unexpected performance by the twenty defendants in the dock. On that day, the tribunal viewed a four-hour compilation of German news reels entitled "The Rise and Fall of National Socialism," a motion picture recounting Hitlerism from its earliest days up until the trial of the men who tried to kill the *Fuehrer* on July 20, 1944. The film was supposed to show just how the Nazis had seized and then wielded power. But its chief effect was to raise the morale of the defendants to the highest level since the trial had begun. The film even caused *Reichsmarshal* Goering to enthusiastically declare, "If they showed everything, even *Jackson* would join the Nazi Party!" (Associate Justice Robert Jackson was the chief American prosecutor.)

I vividly recall the eyes of the defendants blazing as the film showed the days of Nazi glory. The men in the dock demonstrated that they were just as devoted to Adolf Hitler as ever, that they regretted only that their great gamble had failed. And as this broken generation of Nazis was watching the film, a couple of blocks away from the Palace of Justice a new generation of Nazis was on trial--seven boys and a girl, all under the age of fifteen. The eight had been brought before an American Army court for stealing jeeps and stringing wires across roads to decapitate jeep drivers and motorcyclists. Two other defendants, both boys, had been hospitalized.

Having shown the film, the prosecution presented evidence of Germany's vast slave-labor activities during the war. Prosecutor Dodd spotlighted two of the great villains of the Nazis' mass-murder and slave-labor programs. They were Ukrainian Overlord Erich Koch and Polish Overlord Hans Frank.

When the Russians had swept into the Ukrainian town of Rovno on February 5, 1944, they had hoped to capture Koch in his marble palace, filled as it was with the loot stolen from a hundred Ukrainian towns. By that time, however, he had escaped. For twenty-two months, Allied troops and the Russians had hunted in vain for him. Indeed, the Russians probably hated him more than any other man on earth, Hitler included.

"I will squeeze everything I can out of this country," Koch as Overlord had once declared in a speech. "*We* are the master race. We must remember that the lowest German worker is racially and biologically a thousand times more valuable than the population here."

I took a short break from the Trials to spend Christmas 1945 in Prague. AP correspondent George Tucker and I left Nuremberg by car early on the morning of December 21. Prague was only about six hours away. Our trip was pleasant, the countryside beautiful, all the way from snow-covered Bavaria up into the edge of the Carpathian Mountains, the Sudetenland, to Pilsen, then on to Prague itself. It was extremely interesting driving through the Sudetenland, which had been one of the prime reasons for the last war--Germany's greed for it.

Prague was a lovely old city, one of the most beautiful, I think, I had seen in the whole of Europe. It had suffered little damage in the war. About the only real sign of combat was the numerous crosses bearing flowers, crosses in memory of Czechs who had died. Food at the time was very scarce. In fact, even though we were staying at the leading hotel in the city, we could not eat there, but had to take Army "Ten-in-Ones," which we cooked ourselves. "Ten-in-Ones" were a case of food packed to feed ten men for an entire day. It was a well-balanced ration, very good food. It was fun cooking it over the little electric hot-plates we found in Europe.

A Czech family invited George and me to Christmas dinner. It was very enjoyable, complete with a Christmas tree and everything. It was the custom in Czechoslovakia to eat fish and fish only on Christmas. But it was almost impossible to find fish in Prague at that time. So the Czech family had gone fishing in the Vltava River for days to catch Christmas dinner. They finally caught a huge carp about a week before the holiday. Then they kept it alive in a bathtub until Christmas Eve so that it would be freshly killed, as was the custom. And it was delicious.

George and I then drove back to Nuremberg. On the way, we passed a flock of great white geese, and stopped at the nearest house. A family rushed out. Then with signs, signals, motions, a few words of German, and a few syllables of Czech, we made a bargain, buying a goose in exchange for a carton of cigarettes and can of corned beef. We stuffed the goose into a towsack, put it in the back of the car, and brought it to Nuremberg with us. The following Friday, after lengthy negotiations with the kitchen staff at the castle where the press camp was staying, we cooked the dinner in old-fashioned style.

They turned the kitchen over to me. And with the help of many well-meaning people, I baked the goose with homemade dressing, giblet gravy, creamed potatoes, English peas, and real live apple pie. It had been so long since I'd done anything like that! It really had been a very nice Christmas.

On December 30, documents presented at the Trials showed that Hitler had pledged the German nation to an unending fight against "international Jewry," and hoped the war would continue after his suicide. The documents were among those seized by American and British intelligence agents in a raid on a Nazi hideout in a Bavarian village. Hitler's testament had been discovered in a battered old suitcase, hidden by a Nazi underling who had fled Berlin after the *Fuehrer's* suicide.

"It is not true that I or anybody else in Germany wanted war in 1939," he declared. "It was desired and provoked by those international statesmen who were either of Jewish origin or who worked in Jewish interests. I never desired that after the first terrible World War a second war should arise against England, or even against America."

He then named the men he wanted to assume leadership, a cabinet which would fight to the death. Significantly, he entirely ignored his one-time heir-apparent, the burly Goering, who at that moment had been waiting in Berchtesgaden for an opportunity to seize power and surrender to the Allies. Hitler instead bestowed the leadership of the Reich on Admiral Doenitz, who proclaimed himself chancellor after the deaths in Berlin of both Hitler and Propaganda Minister Goebbels. Doenitz thereupon surrendered to the Allies.

"I have decided to remain in Berlin and choose death voluntarily," Hitler wrote, portraying himself as a martyr. "I shall not fall into the hands of the enemy, who requires a new spectacle, presented by the Jews, to divert their hysterical masses."

He depicted his mistress-bride, Eva Braun, as a faithful wife who "will go to her death with me at her own wish as my wife."

An affidavit by Herbert Friedrich Graebe was submitted to the War Crimes Tribunal by the American prosecution on January 2, 1946. Graebe was living by that time in America. But in 1942, he had been the manager of a construction firm in the Soviet Ukraine. In his affidavit, Graebe described the Nazi pogroms he had witnessed in Rovno in July 1942 and in Dubno in October of the same year.

In Dubno, he said, the Germans had piled their victims into a mass grave, then machine-gunned them. He estimated that 1,500 were killed daily.

"The people got off the trucks and undressed on the orders of an SS man wielding a dog whip," Graebe recalled. "Without screaming or weeping, these people undressed and stood around in family groups, kissed each other, said their farewells, then waited for the SS man who stood near a pit thirty meters long and three meters deep. During a period of fifteen minutes, I heard none of the victims utter a complaint or plea for mercy.

"In a tremendous grave, other people were closely wedged together, lying on top of each other. Nearly all had blood running from their heads over their shoulders. Some were still moving. An SS man sat on the edge of the narrow end of the pit, his feet dangling into it. He had a tommy gun on his knees and was smoking a cigarette. The naked people went down into the pit and climbed over the heads of people lying there to the place the SS man directed them. Then I heard a series of shots. The next batch by that time was already approaching."

No screaming. No weeping. A little boy cooed with delight. A couple watched him with tears in their eyes. Another boy, ten years old, fought back tears while his father talked to him reassuringly, softly. Then they all went to their deaths in the same way--naked, body piled on body, the old and young together. As undignified a death as the Nazis sought to make it, the victims gave it a dignity all their own. That, Graebe explained, was a Nazi pogrom.

On January 3, Maj. Gen. Otto Ohlendorf testified before the war crimes tribunal. As one of Heinrich Himmler's hatchetmen, Ohlendorf admitted that he had supervised the execution of 90,000 Jews and Russian officials in 1941 and 1942 under Adolf Hitler's orders. He said the rate of executions had been accelerated to relieve the housing shortage.

The sharp-faced general, pale but coldly efficient, testified that he had commanded Einsatz D, one of four execution forces sent to the eastern front to execute Hitler's personal orders for liquidation of all Jews and Soviet political commissars. With almost professional jealousy, he admitted that his record of 90,000 executions was "materially smaller" than the totals reported by the other three groups. He claimed that the scores of the other three groups had been exaggerated.

The faces of several prisoners flushed during Ohlendorf's testimony. Joachim von Ribbentrop snarled to his neighbors, and Hermann Goering started disapprovingly as the Einsatz commander described the cold-blooded organization of mass murders. Ohlendorf admitted that he had personally been present at the executions. He said his task force had collected Jews in assigned areas on the pretext that they were to be relocated. They were then taken to the execution site, which was usually an anti-tank ditch or natural gully. The victims were treated humanely, he said, by keeping them ignorant of their fate until the very moment of their deaths. Executions, he explained, were carried out "in military fashion."

John Amen, American assistant prosecutor examining Ohlendorf, then turned the questioning over to assistant Soviet prosecutor Pokrovsky. The Soviet colonel asked Ohlendorf who had ordered him to attend the executions. Ohlendorf replied that he had gone on his own initiative to be certain that his orders were being properly carried out, that the executions were performed in a manner that would "avoid emotional disturbances."

He testified that relatively few victims were killed in gas vans, although Himmler had specified that women and children were to be so executed, thus "spared the spiritual disturbances of mass execution." He further stated that the gas van method spared his killing units--"who were mostly married"--the task of personally shooting women and children. The gas vans, he insisted, caused a painless death.

More than two weeks after Ohlendorf's testimony was presented to the Tribunal, French prosecutor Jacques Bernard Hertzog described how Germany had planned the permanent enslavement of foreign workers deported to the Reich. Hertzog explained how Nazi Propaganda Minister Goebbels had in a meeting of September 1942 advocated working slave laborers to death as the best means of exterminating "unwanted races"--Jews, gypsies, and weaker workers. Poles sentenced to long terms of imprisonment and Germans sentenced to life were also to be wiped out.

I was covering the Trials in a live broadcast for CBS when the accused finally pleaded. I'd never been good at ad-libbing. The defendants approached the microphone to plead guilty or not guilty. Then came Hess's turn. He was very cocky, very arrogant. I was about to continue ad-libbing, expecting him to give me something to comment on. Instead, he came down from the dock, walked across the courtroom, held the microphone to his mouth, said, *"Nein!"*, turned on his heel, and returned to his seat. That was it. I could think of nothing whatsoever to say. The Trials themselves soon came to an end.

But not without a final moment of drama. Correspondents heard the report of a "kiss of death" as the cause of *Reichsmarshal* Goering's unexpected suicide in his prison cell on the night of October 15. He had swallowed poison that had been concealed in a metal capsule. It resembled the capsule found near Himmler after his own suicide. Many thought Goering's wife, Emmy, may have transferred the capsule from her mouth to his when they kissed during their meeting several days prior to his death. But prison authorities said Frau Goering had not been permitted to kiss her husband, that a thick plate-glass screen had separated them.

No one ever discovered exactly how Goering had obtained the poison. In any case, he had escaped the hangman's noose. Justice Jackson said the day after the suicide that the real significance of Goering's self-inflicted death lay in its effect on the German people, because the Number One Nazi was the only one of the Nuremberg defendants whom posterity could have viewed as a martyr. "The gallows," Jackson said, "offered him the most effective platform from which to impress his sympathizers with the depth of his conviction and his selflessness for the cause."

The Nuremberg Trials made a great impression on me, even though most newspaper readers soon lost interest in them. The Trials themselves were quickly overshadowed by other news stories--Russian troops marching through Iran, for example, and the great railroad strike at home. But I thought then and still think that the Trials were extremely important.

I tried very hard not to side with the underdog, which was my natural tendency. It wasn't difficult for me to be unsympathetic to the defendants after I'd seen who these Nazis were and what they'd done. They themselves had often been unsympathetic figures during the Trials. I clearly recall the time Justice Jackson turned to the bench for help because the defendants were berating him so that he couldn't proceed with his questioning. It was truly shocking to see the prosecutor pleading for help from the bench because of harassment from defendants who had been responsible for such bestial crimes. But in spite of incidents such as these, I increasingly saw that there were two sides to every question--even this one.

In the early days of Nazism, there had been thousands of opportunities, thousands of instances when *we*--England, the US, France, or almost any other country in the world-- could have stepped in and put a thumb-squash on Hitler. But we didn't do it. Everyone of us had kept playing him and the Nazis for everything they were worth. I thought there was something wrong with a trial that begins with the conviction that *you* are right, completely and wholly, and that you are right not because of might but because justice and morality are on your side. And then four months later, you begin to doubt whether you were as perfect on all counts as you had originally thought, and whether the other side was really one hundred per cent rotten, mean, and vile.

Every war correspondent at these Trials had seen things our own troops had done and that our own commanders had ordered which certainly--on the basis of this process-- would have been classified as war crimes, as "crimes against humanity," even as atrocities. I had seen the ruins of Dresden with my own eyes. That didn't excuse the Nazis, of course, who had practiced destruction on a scale seldom seen in modern times. But it certainly did force you to look honestly at *yourself* in the mirror.

No, it really wasn't the Germans we had fought. It was an ideology, which in that particular case happened to be called Nazism. And I thought then, and still think, that it really didn't matter, it was all the same, whether you called it Nazism, or fascism, or Communism, or the Peronistas in Argentina, or the Ku Klux Klan, or the British army in Greece. It was *all* bad. And it was all around us. Yet there had to be some way, I thought, that mankind could rid itself of that ideology under whatever name it went. We just had to do it if we were to have peace for any length of time.

While I was covering the Trials for UP, I received a clipping from the *Woman's Home Companion*. It was a poll taken of housewives asking them if they thought there would be another war, and if so, when and with whom. Five out of six respondents replied that in their opinion the United States would go to war with Russia within the next ten to fifteen years. To me, one of the most disheartening things at Nuremberg had been the frequency and matter-of-fact manner in which almost everyone spoke of the next war with Russia. Months before I'd even arrived in Nuremberg, I had been disheartened by this view. In Nuremberg, as well as Berlin, we Americans met and mingled with Russians every day. We ate with them, joked with them, and laughed with them while we all covered the same story. Meanwhile, every one of us was thinking what we would do when the Third World War came.

This was one of the greatest dangers I believed people at that time had to avoid. Everyone was increasingly anticipating a war with Russia. Even the Nazi defendants were joking among themselves as to how long it would be before we all changed places in the courtroom. But one of the most significant and disappointing statements I'd heard on the subject came not from the Germans, but from W. Averell Harriman, former American ambassador to the Soviet Union. Harriman had stated in an off-the-record press conference, "I don't think we'll have a war with Russia. Russia can't afford it just now."

Not a single word about cooperating or collaborating to build a new and better world. Not a word about reaching some kind of lasting understanding. Only the statement that Russia on the home front had scraped too thin to go into a war so soon. At the time, I thought Harriman was wrong. I believed that Russia was just as ready for a war as we were--perhaps more so. I thought it extremely dangerous to count on her unpreparedness and home-front difficulties to keep us out of a war. Remember, we were demobilizing our troops much faster than was the victorious Red Army.

Of course, there was much criticism of the Trials, even in Germany itself. I felt at the time that the Germans were *not* beaten, not by any means. Their cities may have been rubble, their lives unbelievably dreary and difficult. The mere task of staying warm had become a full-time job for many of them. They had been brought to their knees. But the moment they had a chance, I thought, they would assuredly rise again. And that would become a crisis not simply for us, but for the rest of the world as well.

Yet I didn't believe it practical for either Europe or America to make Germany a helpless nation, dragging its existence from the rest of the world like a beggar the victorious powers had created. I thought we should find a way--some way--of educating the German people so that they could rise again, stand with their heads held high, and not have to live with the voodoo of flags, the incense of totalitarian propaganda, and the sound of cannonfire, marching boots, and dive bombers.

The Nuremberg Trials obviously weren't successful in what they had sought to do--prove that waging an aggressive war, not a losing war, was a crime. As the Trials came to a close, it didn't matter so much to me if the defendants in the dock were convicted, sentenced to death, and hanged. But it did matter if people around the world had really learned anything from it, if other leaders had actually learned that they too would one day be brought before the court of world justice to stand trial, to stand before all human beings, if they engaged in aggressive warfare against mankind.

CHAPTER EIGHT

Berlin and the Third World War

UP sent me to Paris after the Nuremberg Trials to cover the Peace Conference. I had always loved Paris, where Bill and I had hoped to live after the war. We weren't tired of America, but there seemed to be more excitement in Paris. It was more diverse than either London or New York, and was within easy distance of many different kinds of stories. I liked the city because it was romantic and had so much art. When I was a girl in Texas, I had read about artists who had lived in Paris. Even before leaving for Europe, I'd liked art--all kinds. Bill and I shared the same tastes in art, especially modern art, and particularly Picasso. Modern art seemed so expressive, with real personality. And there so much of it in Paris.

It was in Paris that I remarried. His name was Don De Luce, a well-known journalist, Pulitzer-prize winning correspondent, and manager of the Associated Press in Germany. He had reported many stories from there, as well as from Poland, Burma, China, India, and Russia. We were married in Paris on August 22, 1946. I quickly discovered I'd made a mistake.

He had followed me from Nuremberg to Paris, repeatedly asking me to marry him. I finally gave in. I was still in love with Bill, I might as well admit it. This may have made the marriage particularly difficult for Dan. It was hard on both of us, in fact. Wherever we went, people would greet me and sort of ignore him, which made him extremely upset. It hurt his pride. I wasn't jealous of his accomplishments. *I* hadn't won a Pulitzer prize. It got to be very difficult. I wanted out of the marriage as soon as possible, and had it annulled only a few months after the ceremony. I still wanted to be married, but not to him.

UP reassigned me to Berlin in early 1947. I rented a house in the American Sector, in Zehlendorf, which was more peaceful, more luxurious than the British, French, or Russian Sectors. By this time, I was no longer driving around in a jeep, but had a car of my own, a new Buick.

Shortly after I arrived in Berlin, another American correspondent introduced me to Berliner Helga Soest. Helga was younger than I by a few years, single, and living with her mother, Oma. She spoke English--my German was almost nonexistent. She knew Berlin well, knew where things were and how to get to them. And so she became my secretary. But Helga was really more than that. She was a guide, and became a close personal friend.

I was surprised that the Berliners seemed to have such little animosity toward the Americans. At first, I was not sure how the Nazis would react to the American presence, and there were Nazis all around us. But the Berliners didn't express a great deal of hatred or fear. The general sentiment seemed to be "better the Americans than the Russians." As a rule, the Berliners wanted to make friends with us.

The former Nazi capital was damaged, of course, but not nearly as much as some of the other German cities I'd already seen. What immediately struck me there more than anything else was the starvation. Like the rest of the country, the most pressing problem facing Berliners was food--potatoes, bread, milk, the bare necessities. I could barely drive through the city's tree-lined streets because of the hungry men, women, and children out gathering acorns. Five acorns were considered a good haul. The Berliners either ground and roasted them for coffee, or made a sandwich spread from them. At that time, the German people were supposed to be getting 1,500 calories a day, but were lucky to get 800. I spoke with one concentration camp doctor who told me that a man flat on his back in bed would require 800 calories, the same amount we were allocating to the "healthy" German work force. Children had so little food they couldn't stay awake in the classrooms. In pediatric hospitals, I saw hungry youngsters lying nude, covered only with blankets in tatters.

The average trained clerk was earning fifty marks a month. A pack of cigarettes alone cost 120 marks. It was impossible for people to live on their earnings. Money really meant nothing. Absenteeism was a critical problem because a man simply had to feed his family. If he skipped work for a day, traveled to the country, and returned with only five potatoes, he had been more of a breadwinner than if he had reported for work. How could you fine him for absenteeism? How could you blame him for wanting to keep his family alive?

Regardless how anyone felt about the war, about the German cruelties and crimes, you simply couldn't help feeling a deep sorrow for this people with neither food nor hope.

But while this famine and want were apparent throughout so much of Germany, some American soldiers who were members of the occupation force were looting homes. I told my readers about it. In fact, many Americans in Germany were living high off the hog. We weren't doing cruel things other than ignoring the poverty and hunger and not doing anything about it. Some Americans were hiring a house-full of servants for a carton of cigarettes a month while German families were literally starving to death. I wrote an article for the *Saturday Evening Post* in February 1947 criticizing this kind of behavior. The Army was furious over the publication of the piece.

It is little wonder the Army got so upset. What I did was interview Mrs. Lelah Berry, the wife of an American Air Force captain stationed in Berlin. The Berrys had two children--Jimmy, aged eight, and Bonnie, almost three. Mrs. Berry's husband, Elmer, was earning $525 a month. But even with a wife and two children, he was able to put $300 a month into savings because the city was so poverty-stricken and in such a shambles. Mrs. Berry admitted, "With three million slowly starving Germans trying to live in a city nearly fifty percent destroyed, we have a house twice the size of the one we owned in Louisville, and choice fresh meat seven days a week. Since we've been here, I've gained ten pounds--up to 108 for my five-feet-two, at last. I'd been trying to gain weight for a long time at home, but there I didn't have three servants.

"I know there has been much criticism by Germans of American wives and families coming to Germany," she said. "I admit they have a valid reason for complaint, for with so few livable houses left, the American families--or British, French, or Russian--have taken over all the good ones. We are billeted for ninety dollars a month in a spacious, uninspired German-style, pebble-stucco house with an address that sounds like part of a nursery rhyme-- Humperdinck Strasse, No. 9. We have room to 'grow up' to fit this house.

"Adjoining Elmer's and my extra-large master bedroom, Jimmy and Bonnie each have a room alone, for the first time in their lives. Also on the second floor are the maid's room and an attractive, comfortable guest room. Downstairs are an extensive entrance hall, a sun room, the parlor where we spend most of our evenings, the banquet-sized dining room with double French doors opening onto the garden, and a kitchen almost large enough for a hotel. There is a bath on each floor."

The Berrys were living considerably better than their German neighbors.

"Just across the street from us," she said, "the houses were almost totally wrecked. Boards, cardboard, and even exposed X-ray plates scraped clean to keep out the wind but let in sunlight are being used as windows. Scraps of lumber, box tops, and cellar doors have been painstakingly pieced together in an attempt to patch crumbling walls. Apart from the dreary scarcity of heat and light, the German houses have only the scantiest furnishings. The most prized possessions, such as heirlooms, fine carpets, china, and silver, have already been sold for cigarettes, or soon will be."

She did feel a little guilty about the former owners of her mansion.

"The family which owned this house," she confessed, "was an elderly man and woman. They are now living in a nearby garage. But when we moved in, they had already left. I didn't see them. Sometimes I feel like a thief, living cozily here in their home while they huddle in the concrete-floored garage. But other military people are doing the same thing. Many higher-up Army officers and Military Government officials also have, in addition to their 'modest' eighteen- or twenty-room houses, a sumptuous lakeside villa for weekends. There's no shortage of servants. Officers are allotted two maids to a billet, plus a combination fireman/gardener who usually tends the furnaces and grounds of three neighboring houses.

Servants' salaries, averaging eighty pfennigs--eight cents-- an hour for a sixty-hour week, are paid by the Army out of the rent assessment, and will eventually be absorbed in the occupation costs Germany must someday repay the Allies."

Mrs. Berry told me the American military personnel had all the coal they wanted, while for a long time the German orphanage at the corner of her block had had none at all. A German couple was allotted two hundred pounds of coal for the entire winter. The Berrys themselves received one and a half tons per month. The Germans were severely limited on their use of gas and electricity. The Americans could use as much as they wished. And it was both expensive and difficult for Berliners to get additional coal.

"I walk a few blocks down the street," Mrs. Berry said, "and I see shivering German housewives lugging bags or pulling flimsy, homemade carts or the ever-present baby buggy to an old truck loaded with coal-dust briquettes. There they stand in line silent and unsmiling, waiting for their share of the soft, fast-burning, sulfurous coal cakes. I had heard about Berlin's Central Park, the Tiergarten, with its shading trees and crisscrossing walks, and the bronze animal figures scattered lifelike through the woods. The Tiergarten by now has no trees. Cold Germans chopped them all down last winter for fuel."

But one of the most shocking things Mrs. Berry told me concerned the sugar allotment.

"For Christmas," she explained, "the American authorities gave German children an extra one half pound of sugar. The sick dog of one of my American friends was put on a milk-sugar-white-bread diet by the veterinarian. That dog eats as much sugar every day as a German child's entire Christmas bonus. I can't help feeling piggish about it. I don't want to coddle or whitewash the Germans, and I tell myself over and over again, 'After all, they started it. They asked for it.'

"But I keep wondering how this sort of occupation can teach them our brand of democracy. Several times I've taken the German streetcar. The trip back is no fun. Laden with bulky packages of meat, vegetables, and clanking bottles of milk which always tower over the tops of the sacks, you are a fine target for bitterness. At such times I have no doubt what they must really think of us. They hate us."

She concluded her interview with the statement, "After all, the task of finally eradicating Hitlerism is one of education, and the American women here should be able to show the Germans how we live in America better than anyone else."

The abuses Mrs. Berry described were, in my opinion, outrageous, whether the Army thought so or not. That's why I interviewed her for the *Saturday Evening Post*. Millions of Europeans were looking to America for help, and we were evading a responsibility that was in reality frightening. We were truly behaving like conquerors--not friends. The Army didn't like my reporting this, and tried everything it could to get me out of Germany. I didn't care. The Army couldn't deny the truth of my interview with Lelah Berry--it just didn't want the facts reported. That really *was* a poor example of democracy in action.

Naturally, the Russians were exploiting this situation to the fullest, using the powerful Berlin radio station, which had previously been used so effectively by Dr. Goebbels, to "sell" Communism as the quickest road to recovery. The Russians offered jobs, food, clothing. They offered organization and a program. One young German, a former member of the *Hitler Jugend*, bluntly told me, "You Americans think you can get everything for cigarettes and a bar of chocolate. Maybe some of these *fräuleins* fall for that, but not me and not my kind. The Russians have permitted us to form a new youth organization of our own. The *Freie Deutsche Jugend* has better organization than the *Hitler Jugend. We've* got real democracy--a new flag, new songs, and leaders who know what they're talking about. *That's* what German youth needs. Not your Coca Cola and candy."

A former member of the SS said, "No, you Americans can't talk to me about the 'big bad Russians,' not after I've seen Dresden, my hometown, all in ruins from your air raids. Three hundred thousand people killed in one night. And you try to tell us that the SS and the Russians are inhuman!"

Yes, we were losing the "Battle of Europe" to the Communists. The Russian press in Berlin abetted this by blasting the West whenever it could. The Russian media blamed the United States for the wretched state of devastated Germany. What really did we have to offer the Germans other than candy bars, cigarettes, and Coca Cola? We had banned their books, yet had failed to furnish others to replace them. German children couldn't even go to school because of fuel shortages during the winter months. We were shipping a great deal of food into Germany, while the Russians were shipping food out. But the food we were sending simply wasn't enough. And so it seemed crystal clear to me that America was going to have to actively "sell" democracy to the Germans if it did not want to lose the Cold War to the Russians. And no, it still wasn't too late to turn the tide.

I urged my readers, urged audiences I appeared before to let Congress know that we *were* going to win the "Battle of Europe," that democracy--not totalitarianism--was going to triumph. I, who had once so hated the Germans, now recommended that Americans send *immediate* help through the Red Cross, churches, and Care. I proposed that we help establish schools for German youngsters, that we supply them with books *and* with food so they could stay awake in class. I thought we should do all we could to help revise the German currency system. Inflation and the black market had made living conditions absolutely unbearable. An ordinary dress cost 10,000 marks, equivalent to ten years' wages of the average German working woman.

Yes, we *had* to do more, and we had to do it right away, not next year. And our Marshall Plan helped do it.

I had other interesting stories while I was in Berlin. Once, I wanted to find out what would happen to an American after dark in the Soviet Sector, where arrests of Americans had reportedly been on the rise. So one midnight I drove fifteen miles through the unlighted, bombed-out city streets with an American photographer to the Berlin Mitte police precinct station, one of the biggest and busiest in the city.

We didn't know at first that after we'd crossed into the Russian Sector we'd been followed by the German chief Criminal Investigation officer, the top man immediately below the Russian security officers. We learned this later.

The single light in front of the station was our beacon, the only glimmer on the dark street. We climbed two flights of darkened steps and pulled aside the ragged green curtain which served as a door. Headquarters was tiny and cold. We were greeted with surprise and a request to show our credentials.

When they saw that we were American journalists, the German police instantly grew friendly. One had been a former prisoner of war interned in America. He began at once asking how he could join the American army or navy and go to Greece to fight the Communists. He believed the Americans were recruiting Germans to strengthen our "capitalistic armies" supporting the Truman Doctrine and

Marshall Plan. This view, stemming from Russian propaganda, was widely held by Berliners.

The night desk captain told us his men usually brought in about three hundred persons for various reasons during his shift. He asked if we would like to accompany a raiding party. We instantly said yes--no Americans had ever before gone with the German police on a raid in the Soviet sector of Germany. The captain said they would be looking for black marketeers, juvenile delinquents, ladies of the evening, and just plain Germans who had left their papers in other clothing.

We climbed into a rattle-trap open German truck with eight uniformed policemen, and set off. Our first stop was the Friedrichstrasse railroad and subway station near Unter den Linden, in the heart of the city. We were there ten minutes. Before the war, the Friedrichstrasse had been a hangout for hoodlums, panhandlers, and prostitutes. It still was. We found Germans sleeping there at crude wooden tables with their heads resting on their arms. A bar was there as well, where some girls were sipping the vile German "soda pop." One of our police sergeants recognized a frowzy redhead as an habitué. Two other girls rigidly turned their faces away when the photographer focused his lens on them. When we left, we had eight new passengers, two girls between the ages of fifteen and twenty-two, including the redhead. Two were older women without proper papers. Two were young men, black marketeers who dealt in cigarettes and crumpled candy bars.

The eight were booked and questioned at the station, where we met the German Criminal Investigation chief, a tall, dark-eyed, well-fed, and warmly dressed man wearing a black homburg and followed by a police dog. He bustled into the room, ignoring us, and ordered the police into an adjoining room. We could hear calls being made. After a few minutes, they all returned.

The officer asked us if we had cleared our visit with Russian press liaison. We said we had not. This is it, we told ourselves. This is what happens to Americans in the Soviet Zone at midnight

But then the big chief suddenly seemed to see us as if for the first time. He rushed over, smiling, and introduced us to his dog. Then he suddenly stood at attention and declared in a loud, lecture-like voice, "Of course, any member of the Allied press is welcome into any part of the Russian Sector at any time." We presumed he meant we were welcome to leave. We took a long, deep breath--almost in unison--thanked him, and left.

My assignment to Berlin gave me an opportunity to observe conditions in Russian-occupied territory other than the Soviet Sector of the city. I used the Leipzig Trade Fair as an excuse to go there just to see what the area looked like, although I didn't have any interest in the fair itself. It was then that I made my first trip to Dresden.

When I visited Dresden, I was totally shocked by the useless destruction of what had been universally recognized as a city of beauty and art. Before the American and British bombings in February 1945, it had become a refugee center for civilians feeling the east. They had felt safe there. But our obliteration of the city had been fantastic. Six square miles of the city had been reduced to rubble. When I saw it, I couldn't believe that we were that kind of people. I was told that more people had been killed in that thirty-six hour bombing raid than had perished in Hiroshima. I cabled this information to CBS, and they questioned me about it. But no one has to my knowledge ever proved it untrue.

While assigned to Berlin, I had a chance to interview several prominent Germans. I remember meeting with

Christian Democrat Konrad Adenauer, nicknamed the "Party Pope" and "sly fox." He told me, "Germany must be accepted into the Western European Union and the Atlantic Pact as an equal in every way. But Germany should not simply be armed. We have had enough battlefield dead."

Kurt Schumacher, head of the Social Democratic Party, had lost his right arm in World War I. Imprisoned by Hitler for his political opposition to the Nazi regime, Schumacher had become ill, and his left leg had been amputated. He impressed me as extremely bright. "We must defend our democracy even against the occupation powers who fail in democracy," he declared. "While the West slumbered, the East created a 'German Democratic Republic,' which is neither German nor democratic. We cannot cooperate with East Germany. There can be no cooperation with a totalitarian system, with people who have subjected our colleagues to torture."

Walther Ulbricht, the head of the new German Democratic Republic, had served with the Russian army during the war. He'd actually been a Soviet colonel, a political adviser to Marshal Zhukov.[18] Ulbricht had even entered Berlin with the Red Army in the spring of 1945. He was unequivocal in his opposition to America and the West, stating, "Alongside our big brother, the great peace-loving Stalin, we will crush the monopolistic, capitalistic, quisling system of the West. We will fight as the advance guard of the Soviet Union, if the war-mongering profiteers of the United States succeed in provoking a new war."

Yet perhaps the most pessimistic of all the German leaders I interviewed was the Lutheran bishop Friedrich Otto Dibelius. He told me what I had heard so many times before--in Berlin, Nuremberg, and elsewhere in Europe.

"There is not the slightest doubt in my mind that the atom bomb will again be used," he said with resignation.

"Perhaps the only task of the church in this age is to prepare mankind to die, to stand by to administer extreme unction to expiring humanity."

Yet at about the time I spoke to Dibelius, I met an old woman from a village who came to Berlin to sell flowers. She asked me, "There won't be another war, will there? Everybody is talking about another war. Whenever I come to Berlin I feel so relieved to see that you Americans are still here. I'm sure that as long as you stay there won't be another war."

Those were the same sentiments I heard in January 1949 when I interviewed one German family during the Berlin Airlift.[19] The Werner family lived in a rambling apartment building at 32 Fraenkelufer on the bank of the Landwehrkanal in the Kreuzberg section of the city, in the American Sector. At the time, their little boy Juergen would spend most of the day leaning out a window of their apartment watching the low-flying planes swooshing over his house to land at Tempelhof airfield. "At first, the noise of the planes kept us awake at night," Frau Werner told me. "But now we sleep through it all. It is only when it is quiet that we wake up, afraid the *Luftbruecke*[20] has stopped."

The Werners knew well what the air bridge meant to Berlin and to them personally. "Every bit of food we get is flown in by those planes, and now even Kurt's job is part of the airlift," she said. "He works with other Germans who day and night unload planes at Tempelhof as fast as they land."

Kurt was one of the 90,000 West Sector Berliners who had lost their jobs as a result of Russia's land blockade. In the second week of the siege, the shop where he worked as a presser for one of the city's largest clothing factories had been forced to close.

"About two hundred of us were thrown out of work when our part of the Brennick Meyer clothing plant locked its doors because of lack of electricity," the forty-one-year-old Werner explained. "There isn't enough coal in West Berlin for anything except the most essential industries, and I guess making clothing isn't one of them."

For four months, while Herr Werner was unemployed, the family of five had lived on the twenty-eight marks he received weekly from social security. Early in November, he got a job as a laborer at the airfield.

"It's a good job, and we're all happy about it even if Kurt's suit is ruined," Frau Werner said, holding up the coat of her husband's blue pin-striped suit. It looked as if it had been dipped in cement. "It's the only thing Kurt has to wear," she continued, "and when it rains, dust from the coal and flour sacks covers it in a thick paste. I've tried to get it out," she laughed, "but it's in there forever, it seems."

The family's predicament could be traced to the end of April 1945. "The children were in the air-raid shelter where they had been staying most of the time in those days," she recalled. "I had left only two minutes earlier. That was when the shell hit, exploding in the courtyard right outside our window. Our room was shattered, everything smashed and burned. The woman next door was killed. But that was not the worst. That came two days later when the Russians arrived. We were glad to see them, for it meant the war was over for us. At least that's what we thought. But we learned better when 'the Russian time' began."

This small, sturdy, large-eyed woman remembered "the Russian time" vividly. "The Russian time" was a special phrase for a special era in the city, referring to the weeks just after the capitulation when the Russians had held the German capital alone before the Western powers were allowed in. "It seems odd now," Frau Werner said. "We experienced the war when it was almost over. The day after the Russians arrived, I heard about Kurt. He had been wounded in Saxony only the previous day. Everyone around him had been killed. One month later, Juergen was born."

Like many Germans of the time, the Werners had "managed to get through" the war years. They did nothing heroic, but stayed out of the Nazi Party. Their two older children never joined any of Hitler's youth groups. The Werners admitted that times under Hitler had not been bad, but they insisted that they didn't want the Nazis back.

"We didn't like Hitler and we didn't like the Nazis," she explained. "We are politically dumb and don't want to have anything to do with politics."

Like most Germans, however, they hoped for a united Germany.

"It would be better to keep the country split than to turn it over to the Russians," Herr Werner said. "Perhaps the only solution would be for all the Allies to leave Berlin at the same time. But even then, there probably would be a civil war, for the Russians have made the Communists so strong and have brought in so many extra police from their zone armed with all kinds of new weapons. No," he concluded, "the Western Allies must not leave. I won't stop hoping that everything will work out for the best. After all, that is all I have."

I left Berlin in 1949. But I didn't go alone. I took my secretary, Helga Soest, with me on my flight to New York. How was I going to get her out of the city at a time of such mounting tensions between the Russians and us? Because the Russians were in the habit of erecting roadblocks wherever they wished, I hid Helga in the trunk of my Buick. If they had wanted to cause problems, they could have. I was afraid that if the two of us were riding in the car and the Russians stopped me to check my credentials, they'd want to check her credentials as well, and she didn't have any. In all likelihood, they could refuse her permission to leave.   That would have been quite frightening for her and quite annoying for me.   They could have arrested her just for breathing if they'd wanted to.   So the two of us drove to Tempelhof.   I got her out of the trunk a little ahead of time so that we wouldn't raise any suspicions.   And we left Berlin without a problem.   Her mother came to America not long thereafter to join her.

All in all, my own assessment of the Germans in the years just following the war was not optimistic.   I thought that even though they were defeated, they had never really accepted that defeat.   Although they had been guilty of terrible crimes on a national scale, they had never admitted their shame.   They had simply been taking orders.   I thought the disciplined Germans were still arrogant, still a people who respected only strength, still the same people who from time to time had chosen slavery for themselves. Yes, they had voluntarily chosen a slavery which required no thought whatsoever.   I suspected that they might well be suited to Communism, which required no burden of thought, and was well in the authoritarian tradition of Bismarck-*Kaiser-Fuehrer*.

Whither Germany?   The West wanted a dependent ally. The East wanted a satellite.   And the Germans themselves wanted unity.   Yet it seemed at the time--so many people believed it--that a Third World War, a nuclear war, would break out before any of this came to pass.

CHAPTER NINE

"I'll Be Seeing You"

I married a third time in 1949, to a man I had met in Berlin two years earlier. His name was Henry Ries. He had been born in Germany, emigrated to America in the late thirties, and become a US citizen. His parents were living then in New York City. When I first met him, he was on the staff of the Office of the Director of Intelligence, where his work had included translating Himmler's files, which were being used as evidence at the Nuremberg Trials. He later became a photographer for the *New York Times*.

Ries was Jewish. I think I felt particularly sorry for him because of his background, and what I had personally seen done to the Jews in Nazi Germany. I suppose I was still looking for some kind of husband-wife team, the kind I'd had with Bill. I was still in love with Bill, have never really stopped loving him. I couldn't forget him, and still felt married to him. This may not have helped the third marriage, either, for Bill Stringer was a high standard for any man to live up to. My parents, in fact, were against my marriage to Ries. I should have listened to them. Instead, the two of us were married at my parents' home in Kilgore after having visited Bill's parents in Teague.

Ries and I had written a book together while I was assigned to Berlin. Entitled *German Faces*, it was published by William Sloane in 1950. The book was comprised of my interviews of Germans accompanied by Ries's photographs of those same individuals. Because he spoke the language, he did the interpreting for the interviews.

German Faces enjoyed some success. *Reader's Digest* published a condensed version. The publisher said of the book, "We have never seen so much information so thoroughly and powerfully presented in so short a space as these pages represent."

After marrying Ries, I quit my work as a journalist, and moved back with him to New York, where he was in business with another photographer. I liked New York very much, where so many interesting things were always happening. I never returned to Europe after that move. Ries soon decided to go into business for himself, and I worked alongside him as his assistant--finding clients, entertaining them, doing the book work, arranging the props. I'd go all over New York in search of a glass of special dimensions to be used in a particular photograph.

We did a lot of food photography. Our main client was National Dairy--ice cream, milk products, all kinds of things. I'd always been considered a very good cook. Mother had taught me. And I genuinely liked cooking. When Bill was alive, before he was sent to Europe, I was cooking three meals a day. And so now I cooked the food which was to be photographed. It had to be cooked just right, not simply for taste. One time I baked six lemon meringue pies until I could get the one *perfect* slice. You were never sure what that slice would look like.

I received a salary from Ries, but wasn't entirely financially dependent on him. In fact, I was making more money from my own investments than I was from my salary as a photographic assistant. I still had a lot of war bonds and money from my work in Europe as a Unipresser. I had invested this money wisely in the stock market, and had inherited some oil royalties from Daddy which kept coming in, although not in any great amounts. Before my third marriage, I had bought a home on Long Island, at Amangansett, which I still own. I continued to do some writing, although it was difficult to concentrate, even finding the time. Ries resented it when I read. But I did write several book reviews for the *Wall Street Journal*.

I will confess that it *was* a lonely life for me. We bought a house, a lovely home, in Rockland County, near Nyack. I'd get up early every morning to take Gabrielle for a walk, and return to fix breakfast. Gabrielle was a German shepherd, a beautiful creature. I liked German shepherds, which are both beautiful and highly intelligent.

I'd visit Mother and Daddy in Texas several times a year. Mother died on November 11, 1966. Daddy died three weeks later, on December 2. I clearly remember the last time I saw him, at the hospital. The doctor told me when I arrived that Daddy was already gone, already unconscious, and that I shouldn't expect too much when I saw him. But I wanted to see him anyway. When I held his hand, I felt he knew it was I. Eyes closed, he held my hand, then placed his other hand over mine. He regained consciousness. We didn't have a long conversation. But he was not yet gone.

I filed for divorce in 1979. Why or how I stayed married for more than thirty years I don't know. You tell me. Women of that time often did the same. I had made a commitment and was determined to stick with it. There was a lot of jealousy involved. He wanted me to devote my entire life to his business. I should have rebelled. I can see that now. But I didn't. What hurts me more than anything else is the realization that I threw so much of my life away. Just threw it away.

Journalism had been interesting and fun. But what I wrote wasn't lasting literature. After the war, I had wanted to write for magazines. I'd written a play with Lyford Moore entitled *East of Olympus*, which was never produced. I had great aspirations of doing something more meaningful than just writing a day-to-day story. In a way, I suppose, I was keeping Bill alive by writing, by doing what I thought he would have done had he still been alive. I owed it to Bill and all the things he wanted to accomplish but never did. I owed it to him to keep on going. But I stopped.

After filing for divorce in 1979, I moved out of our apartment in the city, moved in with friends, then got my own apartment. In December 1984, I changed my name back to Ann Stringer.

I don't know how my life would have turned out had Bill not been killed that summer afternoon on a lonely country road in France. All I know is that both of us would have gone on--together. The ring I wear on my left hand is one he gave me before we were married, when we were still students at the University of Texas. It's heart-shaped, not very expensive. He gave it to me then, and I've always liked it. In some of the most dangerous situations at the front, I sometimes felt he was there beside me. I sometimes have that feeling even now.

The last letter I received from him arrived after he'd already been killed. He wrote one sentence I've never forgotten: "I'll be seeing you." I don't think he was referring to the song by that title. I don't remember the two of us ever hearing that song together. But whenever I hear it--even now--tears still come to my eyes.

146

He was a strange little fellow, so shrewd and sharp and incisive. He saw instantly the good and bad in people, and became so impatient with me when I was moody or discouraged. I know he would still be that way, and that thought gives me great peace of mind.

Yes, it seems like only yesterday when I last saw him board that plane bound for London. But none of it was so long ago, was it? I suppose some of it is better forgotten-- the concentration camps, bodies floating down the Danube, the starving, naked children in those cold German hospitals, the charred American GI hanging by the legs from that tank in Leipzig. Yet at the same time, I can vividly recall the buoyant, boundless hopes of our meeting in Torgau, the Russians greeting Allan and me by frenetically firing their rifles into the air, their ebullient shouts of *"Bravo, Amerikanski! Bravo*, Comrades!" I remember thinking at the time how all that jubilant gunfire was not from the enemy, but from the Russians--our allies and friends.

No, there was no language barrier that day. Everyone was so glad to be alive. All of us demonstrated in Torgau in April 1945 that it *is* possible for people to get along, possible for human beings of different beliefs to find common ground. It is a day we should all remember--every year.

Yes, some lessons of the war are indeed better remembered. We can still learn from the Nuremberg Trials. They were more than Victors over the Vanquished. Wars are cruel to all sides, no matter whether you win or lose. One of the major issues of the Trials was the condemnation of aggressive wars. Another was recognizing how vicious a doctrine of hatred can be. Yet another was that orders are not always enough. Just to obey an order does not absolve you of all guilt. We can still prevent wars by getting to know each other, to realize that "they" have some of the same problems "we" have, whether "they" happen to be Donna Rachele Mussolini, Frau Werner, Kurt Schumacher, or Helga Soest. And we can still put our flag on the graves of those young soldiers, some not yet twenty years old, who gave their lives for you, for me, for our country, and--yes--for democracy.

That's what a group of us did on October 7, 1986. That date has to be one of the most memorable days of my life. We planted a Darlington oak in a special ceremony in Arlington National Cemetery. The ceremony was organized by the National Press Club, the Overseas Press Club of America, and No Greater Love, a non-profit group founded in 1971 to care for the children of Americans killed by war or terrorists. The ceremony honored our American war correspondents who had died "while pursuing the truth." There was a special reason for planting a Darlington oak. Although most oaks shed their leaves in the autumn, the Darlington keeps its foliage throughout the year, just like the unceasing commitment of correspondents constantly in search of the "big story." At the foot of the oak is a stone in the shape of a book bearing the following inscription:

> This tree grows in memory of journalists who died while covering wars or conflicts for the American people.
> One who finds a truth lights a torch.

> October 7, 1986

So many years after the war, people still ask me if I consider myself a crusader for women's liberation. I don't. I never did. I'm just a person. To women who think they're being kept down--to anyone who thinks he's being kept down--my advice is, "Fight and keep pitching." Just

148

keep trying. Keep going on. Don't give up! I've always thought you've got to have determination, you've *got* to persist. If you come to a roadblock, like Allan Jackson and I did at Torgau, you just crawl over it and keep going. Hitchhike into Paris with your own story if you have to.

I never felt I was carrying a flag for womanhood, although I haven't minded doing so. I was a correspondent, a war correspondent, a "newspaperman," and resented being set aside and told you can't do this, you can't do that, you can't go here, you can't go there. I didn't ask for any special favors just because I was a woman. I dug my own foxholes, and men respected me for it and worked with me along the way. We always worked *together*--as a team.

No, I was never fighting for womanhood alone. Being part of the human race was enough to fight for.

Ann Stringer died on November 7, 1990.

ANN STRINGER

REMEMBERED

JIM ANDERSON

BILL Stringer was one of my best friends during my college days at the University of Texas. Along with another student, Tomme Call, we shared an apartment in our senior year--1938-39. We all had jobs at different times and places, and with class work and considerable time spent working on the college daily newspaper, we were on the run most of the time. Despite that, our apartment was a center for a number of our friends, and a good place for bull sessions.

I don't remember exactly when Ann Harrell entered the picture. I first remember her as the girl friend of another man working on the newspaper. But before long--it was during that winter--she and Bill started going together, and they quickly became inseparable and stayed that way.

My first and continuing impression of Ann was that she was a very pretty girl, her most engaging feature being a broad smile, which was more than a physical characteristic--it mirrored her personality. I can't conceive of her in those days even pouting. Her face wasn't made for anything but smiles.

Although she was a journalism student, I don't think she was particularly active on the school paper, at least around the news room. My memories of her are mostly connected to the apartment Bill and I shared. I remember attending one dance at the Student Union, where I danced with her. Generally speaking, though, we were not really social acquaintances.

As I recall, Ann was very bright, but in those days not very intellectual or sophisticated. I don't remember that she ever contributed much to our bull sessions. Bill himself was very intelligent and worldly for one who came from a small Texas town of the thirties. But then we all thought we were intelligent and worldly back then. I thought Ann was attracted to Bill both intellectually and physically--he was quite good-looking. In fact, she seemed almost mesmerized by him, and consequently let him dominate her. She was "his woman." I don't think anyone in our group ever thought otherwise.

One thing about Ann that always struck me was her tendency to be extremely reckless. She never seemed to worry about the consequences of her actions. Memories are fleeting and, of course, selective. But the one I still have is of her driving someone's convertible with the top down. She was not under the influence of alcohol or anything else, but she scared the hell out of those of us who were riding with her. She seemed exhilarated by being totally in charge of the situation.

Our apartment group broke up in the spring of 1939. Tomme graduated, Bill and Ann, who were by then inseparable, settled down in an efficiency apartment close to where he worked. I moved in with another student in a rooming house to finish my studies so I could graduate in the summer. For about a week before I left Austin to take a job in Tennessee, I moved in with Bill and Ann. I slept on the floor. They weren't married yet. In those days, a couple living together before marriage was much more unusual than it is today. In Texas, it was definitely still in the closet.

But I had no doubt they would ultimately get married. I couldn't see her ever letting him go, nor could I see him ever wanting to leave her.

JOHN WILHELM

In mid-August of 1944 American troops had broken out of Cherbourg Peninsula. We were all scrambling to get to Paris.

Bill Stringer and I were part of a three-man group sent by UP and Reuters to cover the invasion of Europe. (The third was Bob Reuben, who jumped with the 82nd Airborne on the eve of D-Day.) Bill was considered the senior member of our unit, but we did not see much of each other during the fast and furious movement of the troops.

As I recall, we were sitting in the press camp of the moment, which moved every day, when Andy Lopez, the Acme news photographer, staggered in towards evening, terribly shaken, reporting that Bill had been killed while both of them were riding in a jeep about sixty miles down the road toward Paris. Apparently, as Andy tried to make way on foot back to the press camp, his driver had been killed in the dark by the French *Maquis*.

I was able to get word to Reuters of this report, and at the same time join up with John Mecklin of the *Chicago Sun*, who was a close friend of both Bill and Ann Stringer. Mecklin and I set out that same morning with instructions from Lopez--too shaken to go back. So we did not delay in trying to reach the scene of the catastrophe. We located the jeep with its broken windshield, shattered by a cannon shell that had struck Bill in the heart, leaving no other mark on his body.

After finding the jeep, we searched through knee-high grass in the pit along the road and sighted the body of a US serviceman wearing paratrooper boots. Mecklin and I immediately examined him. It was without a doubt Bill Stringer.

Mecklin found his dog tags nearby, which had apparently been torn from the body by the shell. We then drove to a nearby division headquarters, where we arranged to have the grave registration and burial unit of the Quartermaster Corps come and remove Bill's body, which we all gently lifted into a truck. We watched the truck return to a local cemetery for temporary burial. For some reason, it was my impression that he was later moved to the large Henri Chappelle Military Cemetery overlooking Omaha Beach, where we had landed just a few weeks prior.

I was able to fly back to London. At a luncheon with the grief-stricken Ann Stringer, who by then had been brought over by Reuters and UP, I told her what I could of the tragic event. She, of course, persevered as the good journalist she was, and was soon assigned to the European Theater by UP. I subsequently saw her frequently at First Army Headquarters wherever it went.

I wrote an article later for the *Chicago Sun*, which ended up hiring me as a war correspondent. I wrote about the "Rhine Maidens"--Iris Carpenter, Lee Carson, and Ann--who were all doing superb jobs. Ann went on to become a staff correspondent for UP, continuing until war's end.

In 1982, she returned with some thirty other World War II correspondents to a reunion at Ohio University, where we planted twenty-four apple trees donated by the Société France-Amerique on a site given by the University and named Normandy Park. I am sure all of us there thought that one of those trees honored the memory of Bill Stringer.

HARRISON E. SALISBURY

Of course, Annie Stringer was beautiful and wonderful. I wish I could tell you some good yarns about her, but I can't because I never worked with her in the field. But as a desk bureaucrat in New York who knew a lot about the field, I can tell you that it was pure joy to have her on the staff.

I was out of Europe--perhaps I should say Western Europe--before Bill or Annie Stringer ever arrived on the scene. I had been in London directing United Press's war coverage, but in November of 1943 went down to Algiers, then over to Cairo, to Tehran, and up to Moscow. I never got back to the west, returning to New York in late 1944 to become UP's foreign news editor.

And so I knew Annie only second hand--at the end of cables. What I can tell you about her is that she was simply superb, the best *man* (I'll say that even if it sounds chauvinistic) on the staff. Annie illuminated every one of her assignments. She was all reporter--not "girl reporter"-- straight reporter. She was a two-fisted competitor. Lots of people thought Maggie Higgins of the *New York Herald Tribune* was the best. They just didn't know Annie. If Ann Stringer was on a story, you knew you would get the very best there was, and it would be the first in the file.

I don't agree with the view that she had any kind of "death wish" because of Bill's death. I think she was just all go go go for the story. She had been that way before

Bill died, and continued to be. She was a "gentleman"--a tough one--but played by the rules. I backed her every time, and she didn't leave any bruises in her wake. She was simply better than the males she was up against.

BOYD LEWIS

AT the time United Press sent Ann Stringer to Paris, I was head of the SHAEF bureau. Her arrival was not without complications. Ann was our first female combat correspondent. She was a tall, handsome girl with chestnut hair and green eyes. I'd known her as an excellent writer on the New York cable desk. I knew too that her husband, Bill Stringer, had been killed by a German artillery shell early in the invasion. Therein lay a part of the complication.

My feelings about having Ann in our theater were mixed. On the one hand, we did need more help at the front from someone with her writing style. She could give us the kind of human interest features about GIs which Ernie Pyle had made famous. On the other hand, Ann was a beautiful, headstrong, bereaved woman. Some of the people in the London bureau, where she stopped en route to Paris, got the impression she might have a romantic notion to join her Bill by getting killed in action.

I could see immense benefits from Ann alive, combing the front for exclusive features. Ann dead would be a tragic waste. I gave her a serious pep talk about the potential satisfaction she might achieve if she could "finish the war for Bill." I hoped that it took.

Ann continually produced pieces from the front illuminated by her sensitivity to blood, stench, and danger. Her greatest scoop came with the first meeting of American and Russian troops at Torgau, on the Elbe River, on April 25. By means of a little double-filing via radio broadcast as well as cable, we rang up a smashing twenty-minute beat on this great yarn.

Ann and I were good friends. Her understanding friendship helped me ease my longing for my wife, Hazel, and the children. When you live on close terms with danger, as war correspondents do, small things fade. Big things take on deeper value--things like friendship and doing good for people in trouble.

After Bill's death, Ann needed a helping hand. She loved her Bill. Having no children, she had only him. And when he was killed on the road to Paris, she had nothing. She needed someone older to tell her, "Yes, I know," and point her toward the future, to tell her she was going to make Bill's name famous and be a great foreign correspondent after the war.

I was able to do that. I am glad I could.

Ann was a straight shooter. At twenty-six, she really was a sweet girl.

CLIFTON DANIEL

I had what the British called a "good war." I only wish it had been as adventurous and exciting as Ann Stringer makes it seem. The sad fact is that I did not accompany her on the drive across the Roer. I cannot imagine whom she mistook for me.

I was more of a chair-borne editor than a war correspondent, although I did cover SHAEF from time to time, and penetrated Germany at Aachen, the first German city to be taken by the Americans. Otherwise, I wrote politics and diplomacy, was news editor of the AP bureau and, later, acting head of the *New York Times* bureau.

I knew Ann--as what American correspondent didn't. She was lovely, but I had been in London long before she arrived.

I hope, however, people have been told this story: When Annie was sent up to Maastricht, she was billeted, for her own protection, in the house of the mayor of the town (or a neighboring town) and not with the men in the press camp.

A love-crazed correspondent, who had both a pistol (which he was not authorized to carry) and a bit to drink (no doubt), tried to shoot his way through the mayor's front door when he was denied admission. I have forgotten the correspondent's name, which is probably just as well. He was, as I recall, disarmed, disaccredited and shipped back to Paris or the States.

COL. BARNEY OLDFIELD, USAF (RET)

OF all the things I thought I might be doing on December 31, 1999, when the millennium hoopla had the world in its grip, writing about Elizabeth Ann Harrell was not one high on my list of probables. But there was this persistent book writer named Mark Scott with a much rejected manuscript in my mailbox hollering for help as he was going a new route and pitching Internet. Elizabeth Ann was his focal point, who by marriage became Ann Stringer, and one of the most endangering kind of war correspondents, one with a death wish, and she worked hard at it.

World War II was her stage.

Right off, I have to say that God is sort of careless, or perhaps just plain bored sometimes with this never-ending requirement for CREATION of "man" and "woman" things. There's reason to believe He had a good day when Ann was in the gray blob stage on His potter's wheel. If there had been something called an Anatomy Award, she would have been an instant finalist, or THE "competitor" with a head-to-foot profile on which favorable odds rode. *Competitor* was as much a part of her as being the object of second looks. With her salt and pepper added, she had her own four-letter word--BEAT. She knew from the moment of bottom-spanking at birth in Texas that being first in whatever enterprise she eventually elected to undertake was a must. Journalism was her "gung-ho," or orgasm-equivalent, and bedfellowing, whether professionally or literally, was undertaken if it would help her *beat*.

In University of Texas days, there was a bachelor pad she frequented, groupie-like, and cooked, did button-sewing and laundry. She was tolerated more than desired, teased, and was a little intimidated by one named J. C. Gresham. She took classes with Professor Paul Thompson, and Gresham was his assistant who had to correct student-submitted papers. He said she had a lazy-stroke handwriting style such as a first grader used while having trouble with spelling and sentence structure. In the pad was another devil-may-care itchy-twitchy who loved risk-taking, not the kind one would take home to mother as an intended, but a rolled up ball of catnip to women. He was an aspiring journalist named William B. Stringer, one of the most attractive, feisty adventurers-on-the-hoof I ever knew.

On graduation he sought and got employment with the British news agency Reuters, headquartered on Fleet Street in London, where Adolf Hitler's *Luftwaffe* gave free night-school courses on warring. He had surprised everyone before leaving by marrying Ann, and was kidded at the pub crawlings where girl names were traded as not only available, but amiable, and willing to turn off bedroom light switches and be under cover before darkness fully took over. Marrying seemed a bit extreme, and well, restrictive, if one worked at it. Ann was back in New York, on the United Press night shift. There is no reliable information that she hummed, "O, where is my wandering boy tonight," but she did worry, and had every right to do so.

He was early into Normandy. Bylines showed him as still a big risk-taker, and then as the Allies approached Paris he thought it would be a great story if he got into Paris before the soldiers so he could stand on a street corner and welcome THEM. Trouble was, the Germans were not cooperative, didn't want to wave him in, and laid him low--

30ed him (journalese for "end of story"). He was KIA--"killed in action." Suddenly, the night United Press desk in New York had not only a grieving widow, but a "lobbyist" on its hands. Every green-eyeshaded editor was confronted by her with an appeal to be sent overseas so she could carry on "Bill's war." The way she did her lip-quivering appeal made hard-bitten strong men reach for their handkerchiefs, blow their noses a lot, and grant her wish.

Odd about war is that generals, admirals, colonels and captains view war as one dimensional--they're supposed to win it. War correspondents are not so lucky, as theirs is not only the war they must cover, but their news organizations expect constant exclusives and beats. After all, the wire services assume a whole passel of publications, go to press every minute, so a few clock ticks can make one periodical more up-to-date than the other when presses roll. That wire service is pleased to have pleased whatever insatiable demanding publishing grumbler who buys its services. And among men and women correspondents there is perpetual intramural belligerence which bureau chiefs enjoy. Women complained that they were being shut out, ignored, not treated fairly--all of which was true.

My first encounter with this BIG time had been brought about when Gen. Eisenhower found himself with 930 of the War Department accredited 1,828 war correspondents from all over the globe. He was one smart cookie. He had done Washington time, knew how the press worked, and could be worked. He knew the American grass roots as one of its Texas-born and Kansas-grown sons. He saw in their competitive eagerness a conduit to the "home front," maintenance of support and confidence in his leadership, and he instructed the public relations people such as myself to include in all documents reference to the Geneva Convention "rules" that all war correspondents were to be considered "quasi staff officers"--rank of captain. Military censors had over-the-shoulder rights to read copy and rid it of "aiding the enemy" security breaches. Of course, war correspondents had to be labeled as such, and could not carry arms. We always thought that was the wisest of prohibitions, as had they been allowed to carry weapons they would have made Tombstone, Arizona's shootout at the OK Corral seem like child's play. When there were 930 accredited media people of both sexes, and the Normandy first wave slots numbered only fifty-eight, the leftouts were reading German strategist Clausewitz, who said war was pursuing policy by other means--and they were going to bust a gut to cross the English Channel some way, somehow.

The Army had sent me--a former newspaperman--to England in 1943 to recruit war correspondents to take parachute and glider training so they could participate in the Normandy invasion. This was the toughest sales job I ever had. I got the assignment because I had been an early-day grad of the Fort Benning Parachute School, Class 23. The Normandy invasion would feature three airborne divisions and a brigade that would land in the early morning of D-Day. Because the Army had not been happy with the limited coverage of first drops in Africa, Sicily and Italy, it came up with the alternative of making some correspondents' slots available for Normandy. Brig. Gen. James M. Gavin, then assistant commander of the Eighty-Second Airborne Division, told me--after hours--that I couldn't let the war correspondents just show up Normandy eve. They had to attend the Chilton-Foliat parachute school, take the training, and do five parachute jumps and glider rides.

"They don't want any pub commandos who might freeze in the door at drop time and screw up the unit," he said. "We've got about twelve minutes as we cross the

Cherbourg (Cotentin) peninsula to get everyone out and down."

I told him I'd had some luck with the men. (A total of sixteen had done the training by the time of the invasion.) But, I added, three women war correspondents wanted to share in this opportunity. He said No, and NO, and HELL NO!

"Suppose they did go," he explained, "and one had a bad landing, broke an ankle. American soldiers have this thing about damsels in distress. So we prop her against a tree, and leave her, the word gets out and stories are written, and editorial outrage asks, 'What kind of people do we have in uniform, anyway?' Or worse, a couple of soldiers are running to assemble with their unit. Each has a key role in the mission. And they come over to defend the wounded woman, causing their mission to miss two rifles or weapon parts, which would jeopardize the mission itself!" On D-Day, in fact, war correspondent Phil Bucknell of *Stars and Stripes* did break his leg on his parachute jump. He was leaned against a tree, told to keep quiet--as there were a lot of unfriendly people in the darkness--and left. Everyone who passed by continued with the assigned mission.

And so Gen. Gavin told me to find a way to make it MEN ONLY.

The trio at my door every day was Dixie Tighe, of Hearst's International News Service; Judy Barden, North American Newspaper Alliance, a US Syndicate; and Betty Gaskill, of *Liberty* magazine. Hoping to make the General's prohibition official, I sent a memo to every staff section of Gen. Omar Bradley's First Army headquarters asking for some kind of backup. Only the Surgeon General responded, not in writing, but by one of his staffers who came by.

"Nobody wants to touch this one, my boy," he confessed. "All I'm going to give you is a personal, youthful experience when I was courting a grandstanding free-fall woman parachutist. She would hop from a high altitude and come down like a rock, pulling the ripcord at 1,000 feet above the grandstand. When her canopy opened with a loud pop, and her speed came to a sudden halt . . . Scout's honor, she always menstruated! Maybe you can use it some way . . . ."

And he walked out, leaving me with my same problem--how to say NO to my pestering persisters.

I started with Betty--button-cute, married to Gordon Gaskill, the accredited *Redbook* war correspondent. Couldn't he get Betty to back off? He said he would, and she did. Gault McGowan was my next stop. He bossed NANA, and was Judy's employer. He said he was short-handed, didn't want her stuck in some surrounded paratrooper situation, and, worse yet, unable to get whatever story out. Judy withdrew.

But Dixie was tough. She was fifty-two years old, had covered the rough-and-tumble Lindbergh baby kidnapping and trial. The two drop-outs only whetted her determination to go. We harangued back and forth for a half hour. In desperation, I told her of the freefall female stunter and possibility of internal injury. I thought Dixie would explode--her convulsive laughter was loud enough to be heard across the Channel. The periodic "curse" was so far back in her own memory that she'd almost forgotten.

"OK, Barney," she said. "I'll back off and keep your naughty little secret to spare you trouble. Because if it ever gets out on this tight little island that the British girls who have been too 'cozy' with the Americans can so easily get out of the fix they're now in, you'll have so many petticoat paratrooping volunteers that you won't know what to do with them!"

Suddenly, nine months later, the "woman war correspondent" thing was there at my elbow again.

I had been put in charge of the Ninth Army's press camp, which at the time was billeted in the Hotel Du Levrier in Maastricht, Holland. One of the earliest lodgers there was a highly respected field hand named Boyd Lewis. He had been there with me during the winter's Battle of the Bulge ("Ardennes" to the Belgians, whose real estate it was). He was there with his Number Two, UP's great feature writer, Jim McGlincy. Boyd would have done well had he taken up with the diplomatic corps, as he was smooth and scholarly. UP wanted him in Paris to cover the Gen. Eisenhower SHAEF big-picture doings. I had been ordered to Paris for a meeting of PR types, and checked into the Scribe Hotel, which was the war correspondents' billet. Having registered, I turned, and there was Boyd at my side. With him was this shy, beautiful uniformed stunner who he said was Ann Stringer, Bill Stringer's widow. She had come to "finish Bill's war," doing for United Press what Bill had been doing for Reuters. Whatever else I was thinking, I experienced a growing sense of unease when he said McGlincy needed help, and was sending Ann to my press camp, where he knew "I would look after her properly and help her."

As Boyd rattled on and Ann looked at me shyly, I thought of the fabled Algonquin Hotelier Frank Case, when Senator Bankhead had sent Tallulah to New York to pursue her acting career. She arrived with a note from the senator asking Case to take care of her. After two weeks of Tallulah's goings and doings, Case wrote the Senator, "I can run this hotel or I can take care of Tallulah. I choose to run this hotel."

The difference was I had Ann Stringer.

She had military orders to Maastricht. That was that. It took no great perceptiveness to see that Ann in the presence of macho males was not unlike a puddle of gasoline, and my role that of an unstruck match. The road ahead was not clear, neither was it predictable, but it was a road I had to take. As they say, "Orders is orders!" She had hers. I had mine.

After the shooting incident in Maastricht involving McGlincy, Ann, the Dutch landlord, and "Sydney," McGlincy was transferred to Paris. Ann left us for Spa, Belgium, where she stayed with the First Army's Press Camp, billeted in the Portugal Hotel. She said it was "more friendly" there.

All clear? Not on your life.

With me at the Ninth Army Press Camp was Wes Gallagher, one of the most respected war correspondents in the whole European theater. He was chief of the Associated Press war correspondents. Wes had come to the Ninth because he thought it was the most likely Army to make the final drive for Berlin. Two of his greatest AP hands were at the First Army--Don Whitehead and Bill Boni. Gallagher was the Number One hater of women war correspondents. I only had two phones, and he was on one or both a lot of the time screaming about them--partly in frustration, partly because field phones were so faint and crackly.

Whitehead always shared his jeep with International News Service's drop-dead gorgeous Lee Carson, and Bill Boni did the same with--who else?--Ann Stringer.

"You two dummies!" Wes would storm. "You think they love you, but what they're doing is sitting on AP's top two stories every day!"

The two mental-defectives--in Gallagher's eyes--saw it differently, claiming that they were engaged night-and-day in this dedicated surveillance. If there were after-hours dividends, so intense was their loyalty to AP that they would suffer them.

Over the years I have reflected many times about the difference it might have made had Ann Stringer arrived before Normandy. I'm sure with those high candlepowered eyes she would have found a gullible courier pilot, would have professed to having her jeep shot out from under her, and asked him "pretty please" to hop the Channel and take her. She made such tactics a regular order of the "beating" business she was in, and which higher-ups thought only great.

She roller-coastered through liaisons and marriages. But none apparently equaled the flush or high of being first with a story often written better than any other male or female. She telephoned me once to say she never really disliked me, that I was just the "house bastard" assigned to get in her way. When her curtain began to fall, she called me from her apartment in New York, and said she had not yet read my 1956 book *Never a Shot in Anger*, a story about the 1,828 accredited war correspondents in World War II. She had always thought the book was about the Maastricht "incident" involving McGlincy and her. She was surprised to find out that the event took up "only a couple of pages."

That I should be writing about her on the twentieth century's last day was only one more recurring example of her outreach. In 1970, my wife Vada and I had just registered in the Keekorok Lodge in the Kenya Masai Mara Game Reserve. On our way to the assigned room, we ran into one of Ann's ex-husbands. He was there with the wife who had waited them out, waited for the divorce, and then taken him back. We made a date for dinner, but the couple never returned. Later, Vada and I passed by the reception desk, and asked if he had taken ill.

"No," the concierge said. "We had expected them to stay longer, but they checked out."

On reflection, what else could one expect? Even if the subject of Ann Stringer had never come up, she still would have been present in everyone's thoughts. In her very last years, her memory became foggy, and she BEAT it once again. No bad memories for her.

On millennium's eve, I think of that cliché "all of that and more." For some reason, I think of Ann Stringer. And when the next century closes out, I wouldn't bet that someone won't be writing about her then as I have now.

CARL FREUND

ANN Stringer was responsible for the high spot of my Army career during World War II.

It happened at Weisweiler, between Aachen and Cologne, shortly before our 104th (Timberwolf) Infantry Division crossed the Roer River and began its push toward the Rhine. Our division commander, Maj. Gen. Terry Allen, had taken over a power plant and converted it into his temporary headquarters. A lowly private, I was assigned to work under Capt. Mort Kaufman in the division's small public relations office.

We had three latrines. One was reserved for Gen. Allen and other top-ranking officers who wore stars or eagles. Junior officers had a separate latrine. The third was for enlisted men.

Which of the three could be used by female war correspondents? Capt. Kaufman instructed me to take the women to Gen. Allen's latrine and stand guard outside to make certain no men entered. I took Ann Stringer to the General's latrine. While I was carrying out my sentry orders, Gen. Allen himself approached.

"General," I told him, "I'm sorry, but you can't go in there."

He looked at me as if I'd gone off the deep end.

"Have you lost what little sense I gave you credit for" he asked in surprise.

I explained that he could use his latrine if he insisted, but that if he did, a female shriek would certainly pierce the air.

"Ann Stringer's in there right now," I explained.

The General stalked off, muttering all the while that women had no business in a war zone.

Although Gen. Allen sincerely believed that women didn't belong in combat zones, I know he had great respect for Ann Stringer. We all did. For one thing, she was feminine. Other women correspondents wore the same kind of uniforms the men wore--pants and all. But Ann often showed up in a skirt. With her chestnut hair and quick smile, she was a very attractive woman. Ann reminded us GIs of the girls we'd left back home.

We respected Ann because we knew she was a tough competitor who didn't seek--or ever ask--for any favors just because she was a woman. Those of us in the lower ranks appreciated the fact that she didn't order us around. Some correspondents insisted that we get hot meals for them or perform other tasks. I remember one reporter who insisted that I "liberate" a German car for his personal use. I did so. But neither Ann nor Allan Jackson--the INS photographer who often covered stories with her--ever asked for favors of this type. Ann asked only that we give her tips on unusual stories.

Ann Stringer was with us when we entered the Nordhausen concentration camp. Like all of us, she was angry at what she saw. And she told the world about it.

H. W. SHANK

I don't recall meeting Ann Stringer the day she was reporting from the newly liberated Nordhausen concentration camp. However, we were both there at approximately the same time. In April 1945, I was a First Lieutenant, Combat Liaison Officer with the 104th Mechanized Cavalry Reconnaissance Troop of the 104th (Timberwolf) Infantry Division. My own recollections of Nordhausen are naturally vivid.

The compound included a large, fenced field with several two-story concrete barracks located near the entrance. I entered the first of these. The ground floor of the building was covered with diarrhetic excreta, looking and smelling like a calf barn. Scattered about in the mess were the stripped bodies of men who had died there. The concrete stairs to the floor above were open, and naked, emaciated bodies of skin and bones were piled head to feet, feet to head beneath them like cordwood. The stench was nauseating.

On the second floor were rows of triple, wooden bunks with mattresses of burlap stuffed with straw, a dead man on each bunk. I walked to the far end and gasped as I saw a man on a top bunk. Propped up on one elbow, his head cupped in his hand, he was staring at me. I thought, "Oh, God! One of them is still alive!"

I rushed to him, touched him, and he fell on the burlap, clammy and dead.

In the field beyond the barracks were bodies and every conceivable parts of bodies. A hand protruding from the dirt might or might not be attached to the rest of a corpse. These pieces were the remnants of people who had been machine-gunned while trying to flee, or who had been killed by our own Air Force, which had mistaken the compound for a military installation.

A large bomb crater--deep and wide--was in this field. Three men had erected a canopy of corrugated metal under which they had spread a bed. Here--side by side, their heads above the covers at the top, their bare feet protruding at the bottom--they lay dead. After perhaps years of suffering, these three had created a refuge, and found the first privacy they had known since being seized by the *Gestapo*.

By the time I left the Nordhausen camp, three or four of the more fortunate prisoners had gathered near the entrance. There beside the administration building they stood silently in their green-and-white-striped pajamas. Some Timberwolves had rounded up a bunch of German civilians in town and were marching them in a column of twos toward the gate to clean up the mess.

The civilians halted opposite the remaining survivors. I stood in front of the first man in the civilian column. Without the slightest embarrassment, he looked straight at me and asked, *"Zigarette?"*

My .45 lay open in its holster. Had the two of us been alone, I really believe I would with a clear conscience have shot him. But to be fair, I should add that the fellow had not as yet seen what I, what Ann Stringer had already seen.

JACK ("BEAVER') THOMPSON

IF Ann Stringer was astonished to see me in the middle of the Russian soldiers on the east bank of the Elbe River, I was absolutely flabbergasted to see her walk in with Allan Jackson, the INS photographer.

For until their appearance, I had the eyewitness linkup story sewed up, all to myself--the only correspondent on the scene. That's the way it was planned the night before, when a patrol from the Sixty-ninth Division returned from making the first contact with the Red Army at Torgau.

To prove they had actually made contact, the patrol produced two authentic Russian soldiers. After telling their story, the patrol was beefed up with some regimental brass and sent roaring back along the pitch-black twenty-mile route through no man's land to Torgau.

Because of space--and the official secrecy slapped on the linkup--the Sixty-ninth Division would allow only one war correspondent to make the trip. Since I was chairman of the First Army War Correspondents group--and was not a wire-service reporter--the honor fell to me.

So off I went on a wild, hairy ride through the blacked-out German countryside until we reached the Elbe, soon after daybreak. Russian soldiers broke out two battered racing shells--the only river transport available--and rowed us across to a warm reception by their comrades in an abandoned German garrison.

Hours later, the Russians dug out a load of food and strong drink--much as Ann described. And the guzzling began. Actual communication, however, proved somewhat difficult. It only became slightly possible when the two groups used the language of their common enemy. But only a few knew any German.

When I saw Ann take off some time later, I wasn't unduly apprehensive, even though I knew she had flown in by Piper Cub, and I had lost my "exclusive." We both had to file through First Army censors--or so I thought.

It never entered my mind that Ann would circumvent everyone by flying directly to Paris and filing her story through the SHAEF censors. Perhaps, I should have known better. For not only was Ann a bright, attractive woman, she was a damned fine newspaperman and a fierce competitor.

Whatever--I was scooped, flat out. What made Ann's "beat" supremely possible was that the First Army censors had put a twenty-four hour hold on any linkup story. So, my story (and, of course, those of my colleagues) never saw the light of day until after Ann's was in print--and on the air!

She was a pistol! A pretty pistol, too.

IRIS CARPENTER AKERS

WORLD War II was almost over when I met Ann, though I had certainly heard enough of her as she joined the gang of European correspondents. She operated for the most part alone--no membership in a press camp with its territory and censorship restrictions for *her*. Ann got her story from her own sources, where the action was hottest and the news most significant.

I first saw her asleep in a chateau bedroom somewhere between the Remagen Bridge, over which American troops crossed the Rhine River, and the Elbe, where we expected to link up with our Russian allies.

Whoever had lived in the chateau had fled the approaching holocaust. Everything had been left to whatever war would bring. It brought a hastily improvised press camp and a few correspondents happy to find furnished comfort available to them, as well as facilities for their reporting.

My colleagues and I had finished filing and were on the way to bed, which involved passing through the room where Ann was sleeping. She was lying on her side, arms outstretched, and sheets crumpled to barely cover her nakedness.

"What a *lovely* good night sight!" one of the men exclaimed.

"Sheets and a real bed!" said Lee Carson of the International News Service. "No *wonder* she's sleeping so soundly."

Drifting off to sleep myself, I wondered if Ann appreciated the feel of cool, smooth sheets against the skin as much as I did, such blissful luxury after bedding down in army blankets, tents, and--on a few occasions--in foxholes!

All members of the First Army press camp were pretty well exhausted by this time. We had jeeped over horrifically damaged roads for what seemed endless hours trying to keep up with the action and get back to camp to be briefed and file our stories after censorship. It was obvious that war's end was imminent. Nevertheless, SS troops were still holding on with fanatic determination in the hilly, heavily wooded country between allied troop concentrations. Only main roads were marked with American signs, and these were often changed to direct travelers towards the enemy. To compound the confusion, roads became a river of desperate people trying to get into the American zone rather than stay where they were to be governed by the Russians.

We had hoped--the few of us in the chateau--to talk to Ann when she woke up the next morning. She was gone, however, before we left to make our own way for the Elbe and expected linkup.

And then she was gone again--back to Paris to file the biggest story of the war--when the other spearhead correspondents finally did link up with the Russians. There they discovered that Ann had scooped them all. And what a magnificent, historic scoop it was!

Jack Thompson of the *Chicago Tribune* and elected "Father of the First Army Press Camp" drove all night in order to be first to by-line the story. Or so he planned. Instead, he arrived in Torgau to find Ann already there. She had flown in aboard a Piper Cub piloted by an artillery observer she had talked into flying her. In Torgau, she interviewed both American and Russian soldiers who had been the first to meet. Worse still, she took off in the Piper for Paris to file her story, leaving Jack on the ground in fury and frustration.

"I did not think very kindly of Annie Stringer at that moment," he said later. "I could have slit her throat."

It was thirty-seven years--at the thirty-seventh reunion of the First Army correspondents--before I got Ann's account of the incident. That reunion marked the dedication of a memorial park at the University of Ohio. The reunion had been organized by John Wilhelm, Dean of Communications at the university and *Chicago Sun* correspondent attached to the First Army during the war.

Ann and I were among the correspondents in attendance. By then, there were all too few of us still alive. We watched an apple tree from Normandy planted and dedicated in a little park. Ann talked of the linkup at Torgau, and recalled Jack Thompson standing disconsolately on the ground as she flew away.

"I saw him down there," she said, "but couldn't worry about him. I had to get my story out."

Colleagues described her as "ravishing but ruthless." Ravishing she was. But ruthless? Ruthless, perhaps, only in getting her story. As all of us who had been her competitors had to concede, she was a damned good reporter. Apart from that, Ann was a very charming woman.

ALLAN JACKSON

ANN Stringer came to the First Army Press Camp like a breath of spring. In fact, the worst winter in many years had just broken when Ann came over from the Ninth Army with her quick smile, charm, and natural beauty.

Before then, Ann had been in some trouble with Ninth Army Press Officers by getting a little too close to the action than they thought a woman should get. At the First Army, we had become accustomed to women correspondents going with the men to cover the front. We already had petite redhead Lee Carson, a top reporter from International News, and Iris Carpenter, a true English lady and experienced correspondent representing the BBC and *London Daily Herald*. For accreditation to the American forces, Iris also worked for the *Boston Globe*.

In any event, lady correspondents weren't strangers in the First Army Press Camp. I think we were still in Spa, Belgium, when Ann first joined us. We had gone through the Battle of the Bulge, and the camp had followed First Army HQ to several locations, one as far back as a small town in Holland. But the tide of battle had changed in our favor with the warmer weather, and the First Army was on the move again.

In fact, the correspondents had trouble keeping up with the action because they had to drive to the front every day and return in the evening to write and file their copy. As a photographer for International News, I would often have a different objective from that of the writers. I had to go directly to where the action was to get my pictures. The correspondents often had to go to regiment or battalion HQ to find out from briefing officers what was actually going on.

To get around this problem, I had liberated an old Ford V8 convertible coupe while I was traveling up through southern France with the French Army. One morning, Ann had missed her ride in the Press Camp jeep, and was standing around outside looking depressed. She quickly cheered up when I offered her a ride. From that point on, she almost always rode with me.

I found Ann to be very easy to get along with. She was still trying to adjust to the death of her husband Bill, a Reuters correspondent, who had been killed a few months earlier during the dash to Paris. Ann was a soft-spoken Texan. But under that soft exterior, she could be hard as nails when necessary.

The two of us spent the next few months together covering the advance of the First Army across Germany. There were many tough times and many good ones. Once in a while, Ann would go off to Paris to cover a story, or I would have to return to my headquarters in London or Paris. When Ann was away, I would sometimes cover a story with one of the other "Rhine Maidens," as Ann, Lee, and Iris were called. I remember going to Cologne with Lee when the city was captured by our troops.

During the advance across Germany, Ann and I would frequently be separated from the Press Camp for days on end. We found that it was too far to drive back each night. Often, the camp would move during the day, and it would be impossible to find it in the dark. Now and then, we would be billeted by a division Press Officer. He would also forward Ann's copy and my film for filing. Ann and I often slept on floors, in farmhouses (where the farmer frequently fed us), and occasionally in shot-up hotels the Army had taken over.

As the advance moved to the heart of Germany, Ann and I started making plans for the linkup of the Soviet and American armies. One of the first things we did was "trade" our beat-up Ford for a BMW we had come across in one of the German towns the Army had taken. The BMW made the trip back to Paris much easier.

On one trip to Paris, Ann asked me if I thought we could find her husband's grave. We knew the route the Allied advance had taken, and she knew the name of the little town near the location he had been killed. We found a farmer who told us about an American cemetery in the vicinity. We were in luck.

It was a beautiful, sunny day when Ann found Bill's grave. It was marked--as were the hundreds of others--with a plain white wooden cross. I remember taking her photo as she sat silently by his grave. I gave prints to Ann alone. Not until now have I ever released those prints to anyone else. I feel, however, that the story of Ann Stringer would not be complete without this special photo.

After the visit to Bill's grave, I noticed a change in her. She seemed to accept his death at long last. Before then, every time a door would open, she would look up as if expecting him to walk into the room. For a long time after she had found the grave, Ann carried a few pebbles from his grave site with her.

We completed our plans for the linkup coverage by arranging for spotter planes from the Second Division to fly us to the site where the American and Soviet armies met. It turned out to be the town of Torgau. We drove to the airstrip early on the morning of April 26, 1945. In about an hour, we were flying over Torgau. Our two pilots found a place to set down in a clearing next to a bombed-out apartment house. After the two of them had flipped a coin to see who would stay behind and guard the planes, the three of us set out to find the Russians.

A jeep-load of American soldiers pointed the way, and we went on to cover what was probably the biggest story of the war for the both of us. When we had finished our meeting with the Russians, Ann took my film and flew to an airfield, where she found a plane going to Paris. She wrote on the way, and that story along with my film was the first to tell of the Soviet-American linkup. The rest of the correspondents were just arriving in Torgau by the time we were leaving. They had to drive all the way back to the Press Camp before they could file. The photographers worked in a pool, so I had no competition. In fact, I never saw another photographer in Torgau while I was there.

After our "scoop," the war coverage was all downhill. Ann and I made a trip to the Zugspitz--Germany's highest mountain--where I introduced her to skiing, complete with a German ski instructor who had managed to return home from the Eastern Front. The two of us even arranged a trip to Switzerland. We loaded up the BMW with extra gas and drove off to put the war behind us for a few enchanting days. As far as we knew, we were the first war correspondents to cross into war-free Switzerland. From Switzerland, Ann was even able to broadcast her story of arriving there to London, where UP put in on the cable. I wasn't as lucky with my films, but did get them in the embassy pouch to Paris, where they were sent to SHAEF press headquarters at the Hotel Scribe.

Ann was always after the big story, and could be very persuasive when she was on the trail. I remember once when she talked me into driving across occupied territory from Division to Army HQ. It turned out that the part of Germany we were driving through hadn't as yet been secured. Our car fell into a hole in a blown-up bridge, and we had to persuade a farmer to hook up his oxen and pull us out. The car wasn't damaged as it hung up on the edge of the hole, saving us from a forty-foot drop!

The *burgermeister* insisted on surrendering to us (all the homes had sheets hanging out the windows) but was puzzled as to just who we were. He kept looking at the car with "SHAEF" printed in large letters. He kept slowly repeating it to himself, then his face lit up.

"SHAEF," he said with satisfaction. *"SHAEF de Polizei!"*

We agreed with him that that's just who we were, and he quartered us in a lovely house with beds and sheets and a hot breakfast in the morning. In trying to get back with one story, we had run into a better one--thanks to Ann's news sense.

One day in the spring of 1945, Ann came to me at the Third Army Press Camp. With tears in her eyes, she said she was being transferred back to Paris. I knew I was going to Berlin as soon as the Soviets would let us in. Ann and I didn't know if and when we would ever meet after that. She walked slowly out the door, and I never saw her again.

Notes

[1]Goering, Hess, Ribbentrop:

Hermann Goering. German air force hero of World War I, prominent Nazi, founder of *Gestapo*, head of the *Luftwaffe* in World War II, at one time designated successor to Adolf Hitler.

Rudolf Hess. Prominent early member of the Nazi Party, named Deputy *Fuehrer* by Hitler in 1933, captured in 1941 by the English when he piloted a plane on his puzzling "peace flight" to Scotland.

Joachim von Ribbentrop. Former champagne salesman, prominent Nazi, German Foreign Minister during World War II.

[2]*Wehrmacht*: German Army

[3]*Luftwaffe*: German Air Force

[4]Mark Scott's interview with Ann Stringer conducted in November 1987.

[5]Axis Pact: Hitler-Mussolini cooperation agreement of 1936 and military alliance of 1939.

[6]On September 26, 1947, President Truman posthumously awarded Stringer the Medal of Freedom, the highest civilian award given by the United States. Stringer was honored for "exceptionally meritorious achievement which aided the United States in the prosecution of the war against the enemy in continental Europe in 1944 and 1945." On April 2, 1997, US envoy to France Don Bandler

unveiled a portrait photograph of Stringer in the Reuters Paris office, where it is on permanent display.

[7]Lady Mountbatten: Pamela Mountbatten, wife of Lord Louis Mountbatten, chief of British commando operations in Europe and Burma, and in 1947 Viceroy of India.

[8]Sir William Beveridge: British economist, pioneer of British social security and welfare state.

[9]Lady Astor: Nancy Witcher Langhorne Astor, American-born wife of Viscount Astor. First woman elected to Parliament (1919), politician of reformist views noted for hosting social gatherings of prominent personalities at Cliveden.

[10]SHAEF: Supreme Headquarters, Allied Expeditionary Force. Headquartered in Paris after the city fell to the Allies in August 1944, SHAEF directed the Allied offensive against Nazi Germany.

[11]Wacs: Women's Army Corps.

[12]Col. Barney Oldfield, *Never a Shot in Anger*. Santa Barbara: Capra Press, 1989, pp. 191-194.

[13]Ardennes breakthrough: The Battle of the Bulge, the desperate German counterattack against the Allies in the Ardennes Forest in December 1944-January 1945.

[14]Siegfried Line: German defensive line in France extending from Dracourt in the north to Saint-Quentin in the south.

[15]For details of this scene told by those who participated in it, see Mark Scott and Semyon Krasilshchik, *Yanks Meet Reds: Recollections of US and Soviet Vets from the Linkup in World War II*.

[16]Stringer's family later had the bodied reburied in the Greenwood Cemetery in Teague.

[17]Tito: Alias of Josip Broz, Communist president of Yugoslavia from 1945 until his death in 1980.

[18]Zhukov: Georgi Konstantinovich Zhukov, Marshal of the Soviet Union and war hero. Played key roles in the

Battle of Stalingrad, relief of Leningrad, and capture of Berlin.

[19]Berlin Airlift: Eleven-month operation in 1948-49 involving Allied cargo planes bringing massive supplies to Soviet-blockaded West Berlin.

[20]*Luftbruecke*: "Air bridge."

About the Author

Mark Scott is a professional writer and public relations consultant living in California. He has been a Soviet analyst with the CIA, a political aide to the governor of Kansas, a professor at Pepperdine University, and a consultant to US firms doing business in Russia. He is a member of the board of directors of the US-Russia Foundation. His *Yanks Meet Reds: Recollections of US and Soviet Vets from the Linkup in World War II* appeared in English, German, and Russian editions.